SIERRA CLUB EXHIBIT FORMAT SERIES

Winner of the Carey-Thomas Award in 1964
    for the best achievement in creative publishing in the United States

EDITED BY DAVID BROWER

To the Navajo People

Navajo Wildlands

"...as long as the rivers shall run"

Now from somewhere in the skies one of the Winds came down to earth,
and there he happened to be called the Lefthanded Wind.
"Although I suppose the two of you only are now living,
still, eventually there will be many of you," he told them.
"With what shall we become numerous, I wonder," they thought;
but instantly he had guessed their thought.
"It will become known at daylight, you shall see, my grandchildren," he said.
Immediately he had disappeared from there.

—WINDWAY,

Yei-bi-chai pictographs, Canyon de Chelly

As far as [Father Latour] could see, on every side, the landscape was heaped up into monotonous red sand-hills, not much larger than haycocks, and very much the shape of haycocks. One could not have believed that in the number of square miles a man is able to sweep with the eye there could be so many uniform red hills. He had been riding among them since early morning, and the look of the country had no more changed than if he had stood still. He must have travelled through thirty miles of these conical red hills, winding his way in the narrow cracks between them, and he had begun to think that he would never see anything else. They were so exactly like one another that he seemed to be wandering in some geometrical nightmare; flattened cones, they were, more the shape of Mexican ovens than haycocks —yes, exactly the shape of Mexican ovens, red as brickdust, and naked of vegetation . . . The hills thrust out of the ground so thickly that they seemed to be pushing each other, elbowing each other aside, tipping each other over.

   The blunted pyramid, repeated so many hundred times upon his retina and crowding down upon him in the heat, had confused the traveller, who was sensitive to the shape of things.

   "Mais, c'est fantastique;" he muttered, closing his eyes to rest them from the intrusive omnipresence of the triangle.

—WILLA CATHER

The lover of nature, whose perceptions have been trained in the Alps, in Italy, Germany, or New England, in the Appalachians or Cordilleras, in Scotland or Colorado, would enter this strange region with a shock, and dwell there for a time with a sense of oppression, and perhaps with horror. Whatsoever things he had learned to regard as beautiful and noble he would seldom or never see, and whatsoever he might see would appear to him as anything but beautiful and noble. Whatsoever might be bold or striking would at first seem only grotesque. The colors would be the very ones he had learned to shun as tawdry and bizarre. The tones and shades, modest and tender, subdued yet rich, in which his fancy had always taken special delight, would be the ones which are conspicuously absent.

—Clarence Dutton

The fact that I never had stayed long in any part of the monument
country may be the consequence of a certain defensive reaction. There
is a kind of beauty—and it is presumably the kind prevailing
throughout most of the universe—of which man gets thrilling glimpses
but which is fundamentally alien to him. It is well for him to glance
occasionally at the stars or to think for a moment about eternity.
But it is not well to be too continuously aware of such things, and we
must take refuge from them with the small and the familiar...
Wherever the earth is clothed with vegetation not too sparse to modify
its essential outlines, it makes man feel to some extent at home because
things which, like him, change and grow and die have asserted their
importance. But wherever, as in this region of wind-eroded stone,
living things are no longer common enough or conspicuous enough to
seem more than trivial accidents, he feels something like terror...
this is a country where the inanimate dominates and in which not only man
but the very plants themselves seem intruders. We may look at it as we look
at the moon, but we feel rejected. It is neither for us nor for our kind.

—JOSEPH WOOD KRUTCH

Coal Canyon, proposed Navajo Tribal Park

Monument Valley from Mitchell Mesa

Across from us a great headland, buff, dull orange, iron-brown, thrust forward from the canyon wall, around it and beyond the dry sand lay in sun-dazzled, aggressive silence to the far wall. The place came at one, the place attacked. One looked and rejected. Then, trying to cope with this thing, unexpectedly I saw the sea, I remembered the quality of being out of sight of land in a small boat, I remembered barrenness, monotony, hostility, and beauty. What I was seeing was of the same order, man in the same infinitesimal scale to it. I began to see the country with a rush and to know that it was beautiful and that I loved it.

—OLIVER LA FARGE

Dunes near Canyon de Chelly, Black Mesa in distance

Navajo Wildlands

"as long as the rivers shall run"

photographs by Philip Hyde

text by Stephen C. Jett, with selections

from Willa Cather, Oliver La Farge, and others, and from

the Navajo Creation Myth and Navajo chants

edited by Kenneth Brower

foreword by David Brower

SIERRA CLUB · SAN FRANCISCO

Monument Valley from Muley Point

"AS LONG as the rivers shall run and the grass shall grow," was used in many Indian treaties to say "forever" in a way that both the conquered tribes and the United States government could understand. But that forever was too often only a few short years, years in which alien greed, disease, and drink succeeded where force of arms had failed in destroying the Indian spirit. Many Indian nations were to find the rivers of their tribal domains fettered like themselves, often in violation of the guarantees of their treaties. In the Dakotas alone, seven Indian reservations were partly flooded by dams on the Missouri River. As recently as 1963, Kinzua Dam unnecessarily and unjustifiably flooded the heart of the homeland of the Senecas, land guaranteed to be theirs forever. The protests of the Indians went unheeded by Congress.

The Navajo Country is not safe from those who see its gorges only as damsites and who justify their plans for exploitation on engineering criteria—often dubious—and who all too frequently ignore social, aesthetic, and even economic considerations. Glen Canyon Dam crippled the Colorado and the San Juan, the major rivers of the Navajo Country. It covered with thousands of acres of slack water one of the most magnificent canyon complexes on this planet, Glen Canyon, the place no one knew. Not even the Navajos knew their wild Glen Canyon country well enough to realize the loss they would sustain with its passing. Now, however, they have awakened to the danger their wild rivers face, and are becoming increasingly aware of the value of their scenic resources. They have begun to resist the attempts to snuff out the life of their last living rivers.

In 1957 the Navajo Tribe created a Tribal Park Commission, charged with identifying scenic areas and making recommendations for the creation of Navajo Parks. Seven Navajo Tribal Parks have been established, three of which protect the Marble Gorge of the Grand Canyon.

In August 1966, the Tribal Council passed a historic resolution condemning the proposed Grand Canyon dams and the promoters who were ready to carry on the tradition of drowning Indian land without the consent of its owners. As the Council discussed the resolution, Howard Gorman, long-time Navajo Councilman said: *Crops can be replanted. Stock can reproduce. So can human beings. But the land is not like these. Once it is taken away, it is gone forever.*

This book is about that land, about what man has done to it and for it, what it has meant to some men and what it can continue to mean, if protected, to generations yet unborn.

S.J.

The Sierra Club, founded in 1892 by John Muir, has devoted itself to the study and protection of national scenic resources, particularly those of mountain regions. All Sierra Club publications are part of the nonprofit effort the club carries on as a public trust. The club is affiliated with the International Union for Conservation, the National Resources Council of America, and the Federation of Western Outdoor Clubs. There are chapters in California, the Pacific Northwest, the Great Basin, the Southwest, the Great Lakes region, and on the Atlantic seaboard. Participation is invited in the program to enjoy and preserve wilderness, wildlife, forests, and streams. Main office: Mills Tower, San Francisco. Other offices: The Biltmore, New York; 705 Dupont Circle Building, Washington, D.C.; Auditorium Building, Los Angeles.

The following is a list of sources quoted in this book; after each listing are the numbers of the pages in this book upon which the quotes appear. We are grateful to the publishers who permitted us to reproduce material.

Black Moustache and Berard Haile: in Leland C. Wyman, *The Windways of the Navajo*, Taylor Museum of the Colorado Springs Fine Arts Center, 1962 (p. 2.

Cather, Willa, *The Professor's House*, Alfred A. Knopf, New York, 1925 (pp. 69, 90).

———, *Death Comes for the Archbishop*, Alfred A. Knopf, New York, 1926 (pp. 5, 55, 57, 59, 61, 153, 156, 158.

———, *The Song of the Lark*, Houghton Mifflin Company, Boston, 1943 (pp. 72, 74, 76, 78, 80, 83, 102.

Dutton, Clarence, *Report on the Geology of the High Plateaus of Utah*, Washington, D.C., 1880 (p. 7.

Klah, Hasteen, Harry Hoijer, M. C. Wheelwright, and D. P. McAllester, *Texts of the Navajo Creation Myths*, Peabody Museum of Harvard University, Cambridge, 1950 (p. 63.

Klah, Hasteen, and Mary C. Wheelwright, Navajo Creation Myth, *Museum of Navajo Ceremonial Art*, Bulletin 6, Santa Fe, 1942 (p. 24ff.

Krutch, Joseph Wood, *The Desert Year*, William Sloane Associates, New York, 1952 (p. 9.

La Farge, Oliver, *Laughing Boy*, Houghton Mifflin Company, Boston, 1929 (pp. 100, 111, 113.

———, *The Enemy Gods*, Houghton Mifflin Company, Boston, 1937 (pp. 133, 135, 137, 140.

———, *Raw Material*, Houghton Mifflin Company, Boston, 1945 (pp. 12, 115, 124.

Matthews, Washington, The Mountain Chant: A Navajo Ceremony, *Fifth Annual Report of the Bureau of American Ethnology to the Secretary of the Smithsonian Institution*, 1883-84, pp. 379-486, Washington, 1887 (pp. 17, 57, 121.

———, Navaho Legends, *Memoirs of the American Folk-Lore Society*, Vol. 5, Boston and New York, 1897 (p. 121.

———, The Night Chant, a Navaho Ceremony, *Memoirs of the American Museum of Natural History*, Vol. 6, New York, 1902 (pp. 53, 65, 67, 129, 131, 151.

———, Navaho Myths, Prayers and Songs with Texts and Translations, *University of California Publications in American Archaeology and Ethnology*, Vol. 5, No. 2, Berkeley, 1907 (p. 98.

O'Bryan, Aileen, The Diné; Origin Myths of the Navajo Indians, *Smithsonian Institution, Bureau of American Ethnology*, Bulletin 163. Washington, 1956 (pp. 124, 126, 146.

Reichard, Gladys: in Ruth M. Underhill, *The Navajos*, University of Oklahoma Press, Norman, 1956 (p. 104.

Singer Man and Berard Haile: in Leland C. Wyman, *Beautyway: A Navaho Ceremonial*, Pantheon Books, Bollingen Series 53, New York, 1957 (pp. 142, 144.

Publisher's Note: The book is set in Centaur and Arrighi by Mackenzie & Harris, Inc., San Francisco. It was lithographed on Champion's Kromekote cast coated by Barnes Press, New York City. The book is double-spread collated and bound in Columbia Mills' Sampson linen by Russell-Rutter Co., Inc., New York City. The design is by David Brower. Layout is by Kenneth Brower.

That flowing water! That flowing water! My mind wanders across it.

That broad water! That flowing water! My mind wanders across it.

That old age water! That flowing water! My mind wanders across it.

—MYTH OF THE MOUNTAINTOP WAY

FOREWORD Storm King Mountain on the Hudson is a long way from Navajo Mountain on the Colorado, but they share a problem that an editorial in the *Wall Street Journal* (August 21, 1967) helped point up. The editorial alluded to the controversy over the Consolidated Edison Company's proposal to build a pumped-storage generating facility in and around the most scenic part of the Hudson River gorge in order to accommodate the company's prediction of growth in demand for electrical energy. The editorial admonished conservationists for not accepting a compromise that would partly bury the proposed construction, and argued that too much zeal would ruin a good cause.

Conventional reasoning goes like that in such controversies: conservation is fine, but why don't you preserve something else and let us get realistically on with our growth? The problem that New Yorkers and Navajos share stems from the very understandable urge to grow. This urge comes from a recent conclusion that progress and growth are good and interchangeable and that both consist of an ever-increasing quantity of the works and numbers of man. It is an urge that is leading man to build a tree house that extends farther and farther out on a limb. And very few of the practical people who love progress and growth so devoutly seem inclined to inquire into the strength of the limb that supports the house that is being so nicely engineered.

A different course would seem logical. If mankind is to be well led in the splendid variety of his endeavors, it is time for those who lead to make clear what their conscience knows: if mankind's endeavors in all their beautiful variety are to continue, there must also continue, in all its variety, the natural world that provides the soil for man's genius to grow in.

There is a lesson in the Navajo country. Here the work of ancestral engineers still stands, but a millenium ago something essential was lost, and the people had to leave too. Once again perhaps man had lost touch with a law that simply cannot be violated—the law of the minimum. No matter how much brass or how many cymbals, nothing living can persist unless there is love, and the law of the minimum requires that there be love of the land, and respect for the miraculous, indispensable community of living things the thin skin of soil makes possible and that vanish if it does. The civilizations that thought soil was old-fashioned exist as fossil civilizations, not as living cultures. The purpose here is not to be didactic, but to raise the question with Navajo wildlands as counterpoint to our thoughts, and then to raise it again, rather often, as we look about us on this planet and celebrate what man must preserve if he wishes to remain here.

"We are fortunate in occupying an area of unmatched primitive and natural beauty," wrote Raymond Nakai, Chairman of the Navajo Tribal Council. "This is a most valuable resource and must be protected, preserved, and utilized wisely." Indeed, the figurative soil we have been talking about still surrounds Navajo Mountain, diminished though it may be by the overburdening of range forced upon the Navajo and upon others as well. The soil that can sustain genius still exists in other wild places, places that live on in some of the old states and in both the new, and in some other nations and on some other continents. But one simple prerequisite for genius—that there be a natural succession of organic variety—won't exist for long unless men of many nations, realizing they are capable of forcing it into oblivion, decide not to but to change their growth habits instead.

The Navajo Country imprinted me a long time ago. In 1939, without knowing that we were violating something sacred, three friends and I made the first ascent of Shiprock. It took months of planning and four days of climbing, none more enjoyable than the third day. As it ended we bivouacked not far below the summit and looked out over the desert as the shadow of the peak reached east and died, to let campfires twinkle under the stars—scores of campfires, scattered over the arid vastness we had thought empty. I found myself feeling an empathy I had never felt before. Who was around that fire, the other fires, the farthest one? What had the winds told them that day, the vast sky, and the sacred mountains? What tradition, being understood and enjoyed around each fire, had kept these people so well in touch with their land for so long?

Echoes of my empathy came back twenty-five years later in Santa Fe as I sat next to Sam Day, not at a campfire, but at a dinner table, following his remarks to the First Conference on Southwest Wilderness. We had all liked what Sam Day said and I was quite eager to have the Navajo Tribal Council, the Tribal Park group Mr. Day headed, and the Tribal Museum help us with a book. The book could let everybody, Navajo or not, know what unspoiled scenic treasures there were in the Navajo Country, and what the place meant to the people who lived there.

Everyone seemed to think the book could be good for the Southwest. I hurried home to invoke the power of Philip Hyde's camera and was delighted to know that within a month—December, after a light snowfall—his camera was there, interpreting the Navajo Country. Phil Hyde made a dual contribution. Part of it is his chapter, "Toward a Sense of Place." More important is what was in his eye and he has let us see. He has been one of our mainstays in letting people know the mood and the feel of America's special places, the eons it took to perfect them, and the endless time it would take to begin to restore them were we ever to spoil them. Philip Hyde first put his camera to work for America's scenic resources in the battle to keep dams out of Dinosaur National Monument. His ability to interpret what goes on in wildness has helped save the Point Reyes National Seashore, Grand Canyon, the High Sierra wilderness, the Big Sur coast, and is helping to save the North Cascades of Washington, the Volcanic Cascades of Oregon, the California redwoods, the Wind Rivers in Wyoming. His list is impressive, and growing. Nowhere, as I look over his work, has he exceeded what happens here.

Professor Stephen Jett found us at a workshop held by *Reader's Digest* on the South Rim to help save Grand Canyon from the Bureau of Reclamation's plan to dam it. We dug deeper and deeper into the knowledge of the Southwest and how to save it that he acquired from his detailed study of the recreational resources of the Navajo Country. His dissertation on the subject is an introduction to Navajo attitudes toward land, a guidebook, an inventory, and a series of recommendations, all in one. His final chapter in our book, incidentally, telescopes several events. John Schanhaar, Marie Rodell, Philip Hyde, Jeffrey Ingram, and Bertha Dutton helped provide the wealth from which the book was constructed. We are grateful to all of them.

I feel a special gratitude to Kenneth Brower, editor of the book, and of four others in the Exhibit Format Series, who describes his concept of the Navajo book this way: "Stephen Jett's part of the text is good description of country he knows as well as anyone. In relying heavily on Willa Cather, who wrote the very best prose on the Southwest, and on Oliver La Farge, we do something we've never done before—draw a lot from novels: *Death Comes for the Archbishop, The Professor's House,* and *Song of the Lark* by Cather; *Raw Material, Laughing Boy,* and *Enemy Gods* by La Farge. I think this gives the book dimensions our books haven't had before, putting you in the middle of the country, surrounding you with it as a novel can best, and, along with the Navajo chants, transmitting the feel of the country more palpably than most of our books have transmitted the feel of their terrain." [Dr. Jett's text is double column, in Centaur; the excerpts from the novels and the Navajo creation myth are single column; the chants are in Arrighi, the italic face that goes best with Centaur.]

The concept works. I hope you are pleased with what happens when what Willa Cather saw in a sky is coupled with what Philip Hyde saw; when the mountains lit with their own inner glow in the Navajo creation myth are juxtaposed with the terrain the myth was created in; when a school encloses an Indian boy in Oliver La Farge's text on one page, and on the other page you see the wildland he is now excluded from.

There are now laws in various lands, including the Navajo Reservation, to protect artifacts from careless disturbance, from the idle collector of things. We would like to think that what this book has to say will lead to equal protection for the land, and for the beauty of things alive on the land, that gave grace to the lives of the ancient people to whom the Navajo wildlands were, as they are now, beautiful indeed.

DAVID BROWER
Executive Director, Sierra Club

New York City, September 28, 1967

Toward a Sense of Place

WHEN CLARENCE DUTTON explored the Plateau Province a hundred years ago, he saw that a visitor conditioned to the Alps, if he stayed long in this new country, would be shocked, oppressed, or horrified. While in Dutton's days emotion about scenery was still all right, today, indifference is popular, and we tend to take someone else's opinion about what is beautiful and flock to the recommended places. Noting this, Aldo Leopold, in *Sand County Almanac* has identified the "trophy recreationist," and urges that recreational development is "not a job of building roads into lovely country, but of building receptivity into the . . . human mind." Indeed, a great increase in individual sensitivity might be achieved if park authorities spent as much effort on interpretation as on road building.

Dutton led the way, and his insight about what would happen to a traveler in the Plateau Province certainly worked for me in the Navajo Country. The traveler needs time enough, he wrote, and: "Time would bring a gradual change. Someday he would become conscious that outlines which at first seem harsh and trivial have grace and meaning, that forms which seem grotesque are full of dignity, that magnitudes which have added enormity to coarseness have become replete with strength and even majesty. The colors which had been esteemed unrefined, immodest and glaring, are as expressive, tender, changeful and capacious of effects as any others. Great innovations, whether in art or literature, science, or in nature, seldom take the world by storm. They must be understood before they can be estimated. They must be cultivated before they can be understood."

A woman we met at the gas station in Newcomb volunteered that she and her husband had just driven through the Navajo Reservation and that, "there's nothing there but little round shacks. We're headed for Colorado!"

We had reached Newcomb, about halfway between Shiprock and Gallup, crossing the Chuska Mountains on a magnificent little dirt road. It wandered in the pine forest on top, discovered little aspen-ringed ponds, and found us a superb view of Shiprock, fifty miles to the northeast. It also climaxed our afternoon with an enormous thunderstorm we watched from an eminence above Two Gray Hills. I wanted to tell the couple something about what our old road had let us see, but they were off with their tankful of gas, to collect place names in Colorado like a good trophy recreationist should, ever hurrying over the ever-increasing highways that penetrate lovely country and either lacerate it or pass it by unseen.

Ruskin said, with the invention of the steam engine: "There was always more in the world than a man could see, walked he ever so slowly. He will see no more by going fast, for his glory is not in going but in being."

Do you see Monument Valley now by whizzing past its monuments on a paved road, taking lunch in Tuba City or Kayenta, and spending the night in Moab? Or are its greatest rewards still reserved for those who take the dusty little dirt road that goes down among the great buttes and who feel the rocks and sand under their wheels and feet? I recommend especially the great reward of winter time, when there may be a light skiff of snow in the dune shadows. This reward is even greater if you have also experienced Monument Valley in the heat haze and dust of mid-summer. The crisp winter air is then a special elixir.

To me, Canyon de Chelly is another scenic climax of Navajo Country, and at its best in the fall. The cottonwoods lining the canyon's fields and sandbars glow with their own inner light, and the sun arrives with that low-angled brilliance that drives photographers into ecstasy and exhaustion. Canyon de Chelly is perhaps the most Navajo of all the park areas on the Reservation. It speaks eloquently, in the present tense, of the Navajo and Anasazi past. Here is probably the Reservation's most spectacularly beautiful combination of colorful rock, canyons, and ancient ruins. You can drive on pavement to its fringe and soon will be able to drive the rims on high-standard highways; but travel in the canyons, where the most exciting visual action is, is subject to nature's whims. High water, or sand quicker than usual, can stall the most ingenious mechanical substitute for feet.

There is still a lot of foot travel in the canyons. The White House Trail that drops over the rim from an overlook on the rim road crosses the wash and leads to the area's best known ruin, perched on a ledge above the canyon bottom, with a great wall sheer above it.

In the spring of 1965, when heavy runoff in the canyons kept even the Park Service vehicles out, many of the Navajo men walked into the canyons to start their spring plowing and planting. There are more horse-drawn wagons in the Canyon de Chelly region than almost anywhere else, with good reason—they still rely on dependable foot power in traveling the canyon bottoms.

The best way really to feel the country is to visit it in many seasons and to know something about it beforehand. In a region where so much geology is laid bare, a smattering of geology is illuminating, and of prehistory for the evidences of ancient occupation a searching eye will discover. The petroglyphs and pictographs fascinate me. We were delighted by the humor in a petroglyph some eight centuries old—with its wonderful incised figures of Kokopeli, lying on his back with one knee up, playing the flute. Some of the pictographs in Canyon de Chelly are sheer drama. The Ute Fight Mural, a Navajo charcoal drawing of about a hundred years ago, portrays a battle between Navajos and Utes. A short distance farther up the same canyon is a drawing depicting the coming of Spaniards on horseback (see end-papers.)

The pictographers knew with assurance what they wanted to record. My own processes in deciding what a photographer should report were less sure. I started out with several ideas, rejected them, and reluctantly concluded that I should emphasize the land, not the people. I had read more about the country, been exposed more to it. I found the Navajos fascinating and beautiful. They fit their land far better than whites fit theirs. Yet, I felt that emphasis on the people would preclude the sense of place, a sense that I think the Navajos themselves feel strongly.

They also value highly their personal privacy. One can try to make grab shots, which violate that sense of privacy, or spend enough years living and working with the people to know how not to violate. I would not do the former and couldn't do the latter. I hoped that the absence of a human figure would not suggest the absence of a human eye, and that mine would be sensitive enough to the Navajo's own sensitivity to his land. This hope was the basic challenge. There were other challenges.

Some Navajo areas are nationally known and celebrated; others are neither. I wanted both. Photographers must also fuss with logistics and I would try to do my share. They also need intuition and luck. I rarely wait for something to happen. I haven't the patience, and besides, there are usually too many things around already happening. So I hoped to be in the right places when the light said *now!*

I remember a storm-lit view of Canyon de Chelly. It had just stopped raining heavily when my wife came charging into the back office of the Visitor Center and said, "Come out and see what's happening over on the rim!" Together we grabbed camera and gear and ran half a mile or more to the edge of the canyon. A shaft of sharp yellow light was burning its way through a rent in the clouds. Still breathing hard, I managed to set up the camera, calculate the exposure, and release the shutter. Thirty seconds later the clouds closed, and the light was gone.

I begin to see when I leave the car behind. The immensity of the Navajo country, however, made working with the car essential in many places. Nevertheless, the times I remember with most pleasure are those when we were walking somewhere—on the White House Trail, or walking around Navajo Mountain into the canyons of the Rainbow Plateau, or backpacking to Keet Seel. These were the wilderness experiences, and the others are pale.

Navajo Mountain was another adventure, thanks again to the primitiveness of a road. There is something exciting about a rough dirt road into new country, particularly if its remoteness is famous. At Rainbow Lodge Trading Post, you are about as far from pavement as a Navajo can get. Kayenta once had such remoteness, as did Monument Valley. Remoteness vanished when the high-standard, paved highway came.

We arrived at the Rainbow Post in late afternoon to find Myles Headrick, the trader, busy with several groups of customers. We sat on grain sacks piled against the wall and we watched the trading process. We couldn't understand the soft exchange of words in Navajo, but we could watch facial expressions and gestures, hear the modulations and occasional chuckles. We spent an hour or more cultivating what Sally Carrighar, in *Moonlight at Midday*, calls the Quiet Mind. She speaks of it as an Eskimo trait, but the Navajos share it. I think we could expect to find it in any individual or any people who have kept touch with what the land is saying and who lack the benefits of instant dissemination of the human troubles that make news.

Relaxed and willing, we waited out four days of rain before starting our descent into the canyons of the Rainbow Plateau. But first we had to go down about four miles to our Navajo packer's hogan. We navigated more than drove, for the road was all too often a sea of mud. Somehow we made it down to the sandy flat below the Mountain's shoulder, and found our way among the maze of tracks to the hogan. We were pleased to be asked in, but the darkness that had begun while we visited was not too reassuring when we left the hogan's snugness. How would you put on film our apprehension of that slippery slide to Rainbow Lodge? Or how we kept moving, foot by foot, grateful for the rocky places that had once worried our tires? Or how time was suspended in our concentration until, an infinity later, our headlights found the Trading Post? This is the kind of adventure that highway engineers seem determined to wipe out, and what diminishes this diminishes me. Whom does an overtamed world serve?

Our Navajo Mountain adventure took on a new aspect two mornings later when our packer brought up his retinue of three horses, four people, and two dogs. Walking down into Painted Rock, where we would set up our base camp for exploring the westside canyons, we learned that the first four miles don't prepare you for the spectacular climax. The trail traverses the slopes of the mountain—lightly dusted with snow on that early morning—crosses several incipient canyons, climbs a bit, and passes through a narrow sandstone defile called Sunset Pass on one side and Yabut on the other. Then the trail peels off like a dive bomber into a funnel-shaped abyss, Cliff Canyon, and its great sheer cliffs of warm yellow sandstone. The canyons that twist their way eventually into the waters of Lake Powell come into view, and the long backbone of the Kaiparowits Plateau recede in a straight line northwestward into the blue slopes where the Escalante River begins. The isolated bulk of Cummings Mesa intervenes to the south. If you look when you are high enough, and it is a clear day, you will see the great arch of the Kaibab Plateau on the far southwestern horizon. We saw it. To the north, Waterpocket Fold, and its Circle Cliffs are partly cut off by the northwestern shoulder of Navajo Mountain. Within this arc you see what is left of the climax of the Glen Canyon system. They still have beauty, but to those of us who knew Glen before it was flooded this remains a supreme act of bureaucratic vandalism. Happily, little of the unnaturally—and temporarily—blue water of "Lake" Powell is visible from the trail.

Two miles beyond the great drop into Cliff Canyon is First Water. A mile beyond that, our trail turned out of Cliff Canyon to climb through a narrow cleft in the sandstone, Redbud Pass. At this turn, we saw the pictographs that gave Painted Rock its name. We camped, and spent one day exploring Cliff Canyon and Forbidden Canyon. The second we went as far as Oak Canyon on the trail leading around the Mountain. On the third day we reached the perigee of our five-day orbit when we decided to walk down to Rainbow Bridge. Our first view of the Bridge had been some years before, after coming up six miles from the river through a magnificent canyon of beautiful rock sculpture and delightful long, narrow pools. We were almost reluctant to go to the Bridge again after that fine, wild memory of it, knowing that it was now only a mile and a half from the rising edge of Lake Powell that is engulfing the stream that created the bridge.

We had been three days in the wilderness, with all that is implied in getting close to the land and letting it get close to you. We rounded the last great curve above the Bridge and began to see tourists. I sniffed the air and—sensed something extraordinary about it, but was not quite able to name it. Then I knew: it was perfume, emanating from some immaculately clad yachtsmen—or was it the yachtwomen among them—busily signing the register under the Bridge. The Bridge looked the same, or did it? Was it only an illusion that it looked a little like a reasonable facsimile, a little plastic? To know what the real Bridge looks like, don't you have to participate in the finding of it, a little arduously along the stream that made it possible, the heat and the cobbles and the water *and the time* that all combined to build that Bridge? Can you merely sit, throttle, steer, and saunter and still begin to know what it was?

I think of the land of the Navajos as a living entity of moods—of light moments and gloomy. Above all I think of color—color constantly changing with the light, color that infused the life of the people who have passed over this land.

Overpoweringly, this place testifies to man's transitory nature—and yet confirms his continuity. That continuity may end if this should ever cease to be a land of time enough and room enough. The automobile could obliterate both, and, along with them, the wilderness experience.

I still remember the climax of that experience for us. It was the walk to Keet Seel, and what we felt there. Keet Seel, the most remote of the three great Anasazi ruins in Navajo National Monument, is about eight miles by trail through the sandy canyons of the Tsegi system cut into the mesas just west of Monument Valley. The great ruin itself is not visible until the last quarter of a mile, and then it seems diminutive. Not until you are under the edge of the great sandstone shell sheltering the ruin does its scale become apparent.

We climbed up the ledge, into the ruin, and suddenly believed we were the discoverers. There were few footprints, and we saw only a lone Navajo looking for strays. The silence was so pervasive that we found ourselves speaking in low tones—I guess out of respect for the people who had just departed 700 years ago. The wind blew everywhere we went that spring, but it was still now. The silence grew as we cooked supper and rolled out our bags on a lower level beneath the ruin. A tiny seep, with a depression beneath it just big enough for a cup, gave us our nightcap, and we went to sleep where the ancient ones had gathered food and looked out and talked, and had put their children to sleep.

PHILIP HYDE

Taylorsville, California, April 1967

THERE are several kinds of Navajo property. The land is not one of them. Land is eternal and unownable, but sheep are property, and so are hard goods, like jewelry, and soft goods, like blankets. Songs may be owned, as may ceremonial knowledge. A man may be without sheep, and lacking both hard and soft goods, but if he owns a song he is not poor.

    Songs may be parts of ceremonial systems—chantways—or they may be individual creations in response to the beauty of the land, to the joy of living. Too few of the songs and too little of their poetry have been preserved. The personal songs are personal and have gone unrecorded—as perhaps is right— but the ceremonial songs are the heritage of all Navajos. Since other men too have five fingers— are human beings—the songs are the heritage of all mankind. The continuing encroachment of Anglo-American culture has led to the disappearance of many chantways. Several of the greatest are extinct now; there is no one left who heard them.

    Since Navajos have no writing system of their own, their literature has been transmitted orally. Traditional tales and legends as well as tribal history are recounted around the hogan fire on long winter nights. After many winters, a Navajo boy begins to learn the stories well enough to pass them on himself when he becomes a father. The complex ceremonial myths and chantways require a specialist, however, the singer or medicine man. Many years of training as an apprentice are required, and one must begin at boyhood to memorize exactly the chantway or chantways in which he will specialize, and often this involves many hundreds of songs. Hasteen Klah was one of these singers. Following is his story of Creation.

The story begins in the dark world, the lowest of the three worlds below the present world, which is symbolically white. The others are the yellow world below this one, and below that the blue world.

In the dark world there were five entities, Hashjeshjin the Fire God whose mother is a comet, First Man the son of Night and of Naho-doklizh, the blue sky above the sunset, also First Woman, whose mother is Daybreak and her father the Yellow Sky of Sunset. Then, there was Coyote, the child of Dawn Light, and Asheen-assun, the Salt Woman, the child of Water Woman and of Mountain Man, and lastly Begochiddy the Great God, blue eyed and yellow haired, whose name means that he has the attributes of both man and woman, and who is the offspring of the Sun.

In the Dark World Begochiddy built four mountains; white at the east, blue at the south, yellow at the west and black at the north, and around them a circle of Mirage Mountains, and in the centre a Red Mountain. He created four kinds of Ants, red, black, yellow and black, grey ones, and other insects, and smiled as he made them!

In the East he planted Big Reed (bamboo), in the South big sunflowers, in the West reeds, and sunflowers in the North, and he gave them one Law. Hashjeshjin, the Fire God was jealous and angry, and after four days he began burning the world.

Begochiddy told First Man to collect earth, reeds and plants, and stuck the Big Reed into the central Red Mountain, and all the created beings climbed into it, and the reed grew up into the second world, while the lowest world burned and is still burning.

· · ·

In the second world Begochiddy created more mountains and plants like those in the Dark World, and also planted cotton, but it was not a fertile soil. He created, also, bees, and a pair of male and female twins, and Begochiddy smiled as he made them! The Fire God killed the Twins by permission of Begochiddy, who took the bodies of the slain Twins and out of them made symbolic figures called Ethkay-nah-ashi and breathed his spirit into the male figure and when he did this a great sound began in the figure, and the cotton which he had planted in the four directions, rose up and turned into clouds; and when he breathed into the female figure the four Holy Plants grew up under the clouds. So, vegetation began, and the created people were happy and went to the mountains to get the plants. They wanted to live on the mountains, but were forbidden to do this, and the Fire God said, "If you will not obey I will burn the water," and so Begochiddy set up the Big Reed again and all created up to this time were put into it, and it grew up into the Third World.

. . .

Pictographs at Standing Cow Ruin, Canyon del Muerto

In this Third World were placed all that were on the world below, and Begochiddy created many springs and streams including one running from the West to the East and turning South (a female river) and one running from North to South and crossing the female river and turning West, (Navajo form of Swastika), this was called the Place of Crossing Waters. Begochiddy also made water animals and monsters, lightning, cyclones, also birds, trees and everything needed, and gave life to creation by breathing through the dead substance of the Ethkay-nah-ashi figures. He created new types of men and women and the Hermaphrodite was in charge of all creation. They all had one language which all creation understood.

There was no Sun or Moon, but the mountains gave light.

. . .

Marble Gorge

Begochiddy made himself a rainbow house and the Five Gods of the Dark World lived in the East, the people in the centre, and Coyote moved about and kept track of creation. The Hopi and the Taos Indians were created then, also. Corn was planted under the direction of Estsan-nah-tah, the Leader of the Women; also tobacco, beans, pumpkins and squash. They killed deer for meat.

At this time the first marriage took place between one of the chief men and the daughter of Estsan-nah-tah. The young wife began to neglect her duties and spent her time down by the river where she met the Water Horse who appeared to her like a young man. Her husband found this out and there was so much trouble between them and also with her mother, that all the Chiefs resigned as they could not keep order.

Begochiddy decided to separate the men and the women, and the male and female animals by putting all the males to live across the river to cool their passions. The men throve but the women did not, and after several years begged to be reunited with their husbands, and that they would attend to their duties and be obedient. Begochiddy forgave them but said if there was any more trouble he would make another flood to destroy them.

One day when Salt Woman and another woman were walking by the Place of Crossing Waters, they saw a baby with long black hair floating in the whirlpool and told the people about this. Coyote was interested and went and lifted the baby out of the water and hid it under his blanket and kept it there for four days. Then a great noise began in the East and traveled round to the South, West and North and the people were frightened. Begochiddy knew what was coming, but sent our messengers to bring news of it. A crow went to the East and found a black storm coming; a magpie to the South who reported a blue storm coming; to the West a hummingbird told of a yellow storm; to the North a dove was sent, who found a white storm there. Then all the Gods gathered plants, animals and all created, and put them in the great Reed.

. . .

Now the hot waters from the four storms were rushing on the
Big Reed, which would not start to grow upward and had to be moved
to a spring. The Turkey people clung to the outside of the Big Reed,
and as the waters rose their tails dipped in foam and are white to this day.
The Big Reed could not reach the next world and Begochiddy
made a white cloud above it to reach higher and the spider people
wove a web around the edge to make it safer.

· · ·

The people were anxious, so Begochiddy called a Council to see what they could suggest to make it possible to ascend farther, and the Locust said, "Call the Ant people," but when they tried to dig a hole through to the upper world they could not succeed, and Begochiddy said to the Locust, "Show us how to get through," and the Locust put his arrow on his forehead and shot up into the Fourth World. He had great power. He came up to the Fourth World through the crust of mud and water, for water covered his world, and over it was flying a great White Bird who was the power in control of it. He attacked the Locust and tried to kill him, and then they both tried tests of magic power until the White Bird was frightened and fled to the East. Three other Birds from the other directions came and tested their power against the Locust but he proved to be stronger and won control. He returned, then, to the people in the Big Reed who were very anxious, and told them of his victory.

· · ·

Begochiddy asked who would go up next, but no one would venture, so he went up himself, and came out on an island in the middle of the water. He saw a great White cloud in the East and went to it on a Rainbow, and found there Talking God, the God of the Yehbechai (Night Chant) ceremony and they greeted each other and were happy together, and afterwards Begochiddy went to a blue cloud in the South and found there Beganaskiddy, (Bringer of Seeds), and later he went to the yellow cloud in the West and met Hashje-hogahn (House God), and to the North and met another Seed-bringer and they rejoiced.

. . .

Begochiddy stood on the island in the middle of the world of water and saw the four Gods standing up to their breasts in water, and waved to each God in turn, and they rose as he greeted them on to the surface of the water. Then these four Gods with their canes of power pushed back the waters in the four directions and it ran off and left rivers; and where the waters had been were badlands and monsters who had been living there, and the ocean was round the edge of the world. Begochiddy blew on the monsters and they turned into strange rocks, and as he continued blowing a crust formed on the mud, and he saw there were twelve Yeh (Gods) in each of the four directions, and they were beautiful.

. . .

When Begochiddy came back to the Big Reed the people greeted him as "Sechai" (Grandfather) and he said the world was good. (Badger went up to the surface and tried to walk on the crust but broke through, and his paws are black to this day.) Begochiddy asked how the mud could be dried and they sent up lightning, cyclones, and hail of the four colours, white, blue, yellow and black, and these broke up the petrified wood and rocks. Then cyclones blew until the mud was dried, and dust devils trimmed the earth smooth, and the small whirlwinds spread the stones evenly. The storms, then, went below to the Third World from whence they came, and the people came up to this world led by the ants. They called this world Hahjeenah.

The water from the Third World kept welling up into the Fourth World and even Begochiddy could not stop it, and they held a council to discuss why this should happen, and they felt that some one had done wrong; finally Begochiddy said that perhaps the Coyote was the cause of the trouble, and he made Coyote open his blanket, and there was the stolen baby which turned out to be Water-Monster's child, and Coyote threw it back down to the Third World and the water stopped rising.

There was no fire-making material in this world except what belonged to the Fire God, Hashjeshjin, and Coyote went to get it to the place where Dontso, the Messenger Fly and Fire God were lying asleep while rocks were burning all around, and Coyote stole fire and brought it to the people.

Cottonwood and petrified sand dunes, Canyon de Chelly

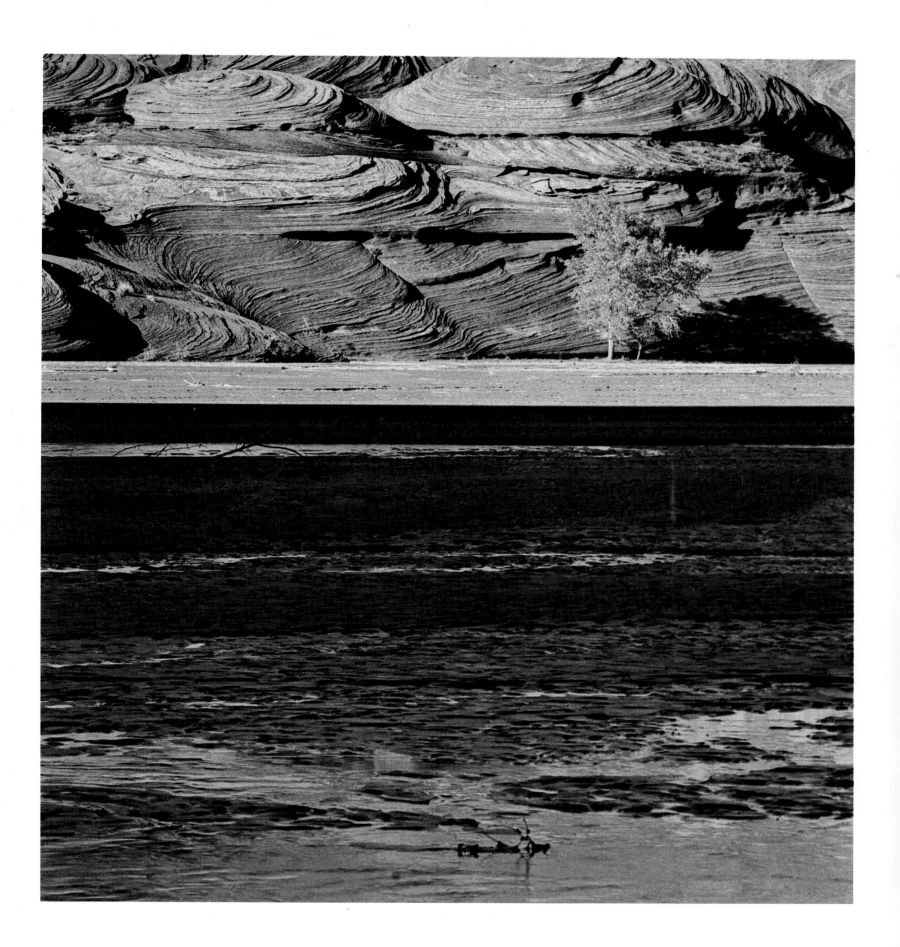

They planned the creation of the Sun and Moon, and many stars and constellations, and they named the months, and gave them the constellations that belonged to them.

They then came out from the Sweat House and made another Hogahn of Rainbows, and all the Gods and chiefs gathered to a big Council, and they sang the "Beginning of the World Song," and the spirits of all things to be created were in the Hogahn. All corn and seeds were brought by the Yeh Gods, and Fire God brought the Sun, Moon and stars and all light.

They placed all the mountains, represented by piles of earth, in their proper relation to each other, with the Sun in the East, and the Moon in the West, and they put the spirits of mountains and sun and moon into these, and while they created spirits they always sang. The two black Gods of Fire put their spirits into the stars and mountains, and the spirits were like the Gods.

Begochiddy told the Council that all these songs should be remembered forever, also the names of the mountains. First Man and First Woman, who have the spirit of sickness and give it to men when they do wrong, said they would bring sickness to men if they forget these things. The Yeh Gods were to watch over men, and give them flint to make fire.

Begochiddy said, "We must hurry and create the spirit of Nahastsan, the earth, which is the spirit that makes things grow, also the spirit of the Sky, of rain and clouds."

. . .

They made the Sun of fire with a rainbow around it, and put the Turquoise man into it as its spirit, the Moon was made of ice, with the White Shell man as its spirit. They put the Fall and Winter in the West and North, and the Spring and Summer in the South and East; the month of October was claimed by Coyote, it is half summer and half winter and called the changing month.

Then all the spirits went to the places where they belonged, and they raised the Sun and Moon, Stars and Winds. The Fire God placed the North Star, and the other first Gods placed other constellations, the women placing the Milky Way and other stars. Coyote chose two fighting stars and Antares in the South. They put the forty-eight cyclones under the edges of the world in the four directions to hold it up, and sent other winds to hold up the sky and stars.

Begochiddy then took the Ethkay-nah-ashi—the mysterious transmitters of life—and motioned to all creation and it came to life and moved at different speeds.

· · ·

The people's eyes became paralyzed and it was explained that certain stars (and a son-in-law and mother-in-law) must not meet, and when this law was understood the people's eyes recovered. Then the Earth and Sky Spirits and Sun and Moon and mountains were named, and Coyote claimed Tsoll-tsilth (Mt. Taylor) for his own name, but they said "No, your name is Mah-ih, thief." He was angry and sent his spirit to trouble the mountain, which was disturbed and began to slip, so the Gods reënforced it with little peaks to keep it steady.

Now, everything was in place, but the Earth, Sky, Sun and Moon did not move, and Coyote said the reason was that someone was going to die. Then the first man died and the Earth, Sun, Sky and Moon began to move, and the Sun said, "I am glad when death comes because it is what keeps me moving." So all come to life when Begochiddy breathed his spirit into the Ethkay-nah-ashi, and he appointed the seasons, and at first the Sun was too near the earth but finally reached the right distance; and the ants began to build houses.

. . .

This ends the creation of human beings and animals. Begochiddy was glad and laughing when he had finished creation and he made them race around the world and the animals also. The donkey won, for Begochiddy loved him most. They made a hogahn for the new people and there is a song which is sung now, just after sundown, for thanksgiving and prayer. After this Begochiddy turned all animals loose to wander. There are many songs made while creation was being made, and he said, "Sometime I will come back and need you."

Meanwhile Coyote made some more coyotes and also some dogs, and gave them their names. The Gods took the First people out of the cave and Begochiddy told the people that they should all have different languages in the future, and they divided the seeds also, the birds chose what tribe they would belong to and learned how to build their nests. The people chose their types of dress and Begochiddy told them how they should worship, and he told the plants when to bear seeds and fruits. Then the people went their different ways, and the last made people lived near Huerfano and are now called the Salt Clan. They made a ceremonial hogahn and the Gods told stories, and these stories and songs were passed on to men. Nayenezgani was put in charge of this world and Begochiddy of Heaven. To make the four chiefs holy they put earth from all the holy mountains in their shoes and crystals into their mouths to make their speech true. The Salt Clan grew and split into many clans which now exist. Begochiddy said, "As I have made each clan and building I have made for each a spirit, and I laughed as I made them." He also made two spirits which no one has seen. ◆

I. Dinetah: Navajoland

For ages and ages the plans have been made.
For ages and ages the plans of the Sacred Mountains have been made.
—ORIGIN LEGEND

ACCORDING TO Navajo legend, First Man and First Woman brought up with them from the lower worlds some earth from the four sacred mountains there. Some of this earth was mixed with white shell, and this became *Sis Najini*, the sacred mountain of the east. It was fastened to the earth by a bolt of lightning and was decorated with white shell, lightning, white corn, black clouds, and violent rain with lightning. Eggs of the white dove were placed on the mountaintop. All was covered with a sheet of white dawn.

Some of the earth was mixed with turquoise, and this became *Tso Dzil*, the sacred Tongue Mountain of the south. It was fastened to the earth by a flint knife and was decorated with turquoise, dark mists, gentle rain, and all species of birds and animals. Eggs of the mountain bluebird were placed on the summit. Over all was put a covering of blue sky.

Some of the earth was mixed with abalone shell, and this became *Doko'o'slid*, the sacred Shining-on-Top Mountain of the west. This mountain was fastened to the earth by a sunbeam and was decorated with mother-of-pearl, black clouds, violent rain with lightning, yellow corn, and every sort of wild animal. Eggs of the yellow warbler were placed on the top of the peak. Over all was spread a blanket of yellow evening light.

Some of the earth was mixed with jet, and this became *Dibé Ntsa*, the sacred Big Mountain Sheep Peak of the

north, in the La Plata Mountains of Colorado. It was fastened to the earth by a rainbow and was decorated with jet, dark mist, violent rain with lightning, and all wild plants and animals. Eggs of the redwing blackbird were placed on the mountain top. Over all was laid darkness.

And between the four mountains lay the land of the Navajos, *Dinétah*. "So in the form of these Sacred Mountains was our Mother made for us. Blanca Peak is our Mother. . . . In accordance with it we live. In the midst of these four Sacred Mountains that were placed, there we live. With that, we who are The People are the heart of the world."

From the lower worlds were brought the prototypes of the mountains, the rivers, and animate beings, which are ultimately the gifts of the Sun Father. "Now the earth, which had been stretched, became solid, and the rivers flowed. Trees grew along the banks of the rivers, and flowers grew at the foot of the mountains with the rocks and the cliffs and other trees above them. The Mother Earth was very beautiful."

Beaver brought cottonwoods to the rivers, and from a stone he knocked chips, which became river boulders. Otter brought willows, and Rock Wren sprinkled rock dust here and there, and cliffs sprang into being.

El Huerfano mesa is the center of the world. The volcanic necks around Mount Taylor are the heads of monsters killed by the Twin War Gods, and the lava flow near

McCartys is Big Monster's spilt blood. Pollen Mountain was once a female giant. Her head is Navajo Mountain, her body Black Mesa, and her feet Balukai Mesa. Goods-of-Value Mountain, a male, has as his head Chuska Peak, while his body is the Chuska chain and his feet Beautiful Mountain. On the summits of these figures stand the Sky Supporters, deities who hold up the canopy of sky. Another stands on top of Agathla Peak in Monument Valley. Between the earth and the sky move the sun, moon, and stars, which are held aloft by the winds.

The sun was made by First Man and First Woman from a great turquoise disc, or, some say, a disc of turquoise-edged crystal, heated by the fire of Hashcheshzhini, the Black Fire God. It has eyes, a nose, a mouth, and horns and is bordered with red rain, lightning and snakes, although some say that radiating eagle and flicker feathers fringe its circumference. The moon is a great, perfect white shell, or, some say, a portion of rock crystal or ice bordered with white shell, sheet lightning, and sacred waters. The sun and the moon are moved across the sky by the twin Pollen Boys. The stars are the people's offerings of turquoise and white stones. Two black gods of fire put their spirits into the stars and into the Sacred Mountains which, therefore, are living mountains; if people do not believe that the *yei* spirits are in these mountains and keep them holy, sickness will come to the people.

The gods and the spirits of the Sacred Mountains created Man. He was made of all rains, springs, rivers, ponds, black clouds, and sky. His feet are made of earth and his legs of lightning. White shell forms his knees, and his body is white and yellow corn; his flesh is of daybreak, his hair darkness; his eyes are of the sun. White corn forms his teeth, black corn his eyebrows, and red coral beads his nose. His tears are of rain, his tongue of straight lightning, and his voice of thunder. His heart is obsidian; the little whirlwind keeps his nerves in motion, and his movement is the air. The name of this new kind of being was "Created from Everything."

II. Plateau Country

He stirs, he stirs, he stirs, he stirs,
Among the land of dawning, he stirs, he stirs;
The pollen of the dawning, he stirs, he stirs;
Now in old age wandering, he stirs, he stirs;
Now on the trail of beauty, he stirs, he stirs;
He stirs, he stirs, he stirs, he stirs.
—WAKING SONG, NIGHT WAY

LYING BETWEEN the four sacred mountains, the Navajo country is part of the great Plateau Province of Arizona, New Mexico, Utah, and Colorado. Unlike the landscapes of the northeastern woodlands, or of other American regions friendly and intimate in atmosphere, the plateau country of the Southwest is, for the most part, distant and aloof in its barren vastness. To some, even those who have loved the desert, it is almost frightening.

It is a land that requires time to be comprehended. For someone who is unused to the scale of the southwestern landscape, comprehension requires waiting, wandering, wondering; for such landscapes are at first hardly believable, impossible to absorb at a single sitting, or, indeed, by being stationary at all. They must be experienced as space, both horizontal and vertical, and as time—or, rather, as near timelessness, for although there are changes, they are rapid only by the geological clock. Here the seasons manifest themselves in weather—rain or drought, snow or sun—rather than in cycles of life. Cactuses and ephemerals do flower in spring, and in the highlands and along the watercourses aspen and cottonwood light the autumn forest with yellow patches and streaks of flame, but the vegetation, sparse to begin with, seems lost in the awesome open spaces and among the looming cliffs and monuments.

This is essentially a lithic land. Stone is the dominant material; even where thinly veiled by sandy soil, rock is the ever obvious medium of the fluvial and eolian architects of the canyon and mesa country. One's appreciation of these landscapes is more like appreciation of the carved stone of a Gothic Cathedral than it is of woodland. Here the stone is not lifeless, but possesses a vitality of its own, partly a consequence of the variety and warmth of the radiant colors of the rocks, and partly from the vital, positive quality of the soaring forms. They seem more than momentarily surviving remnants of once continuous layers of rock, more than just the slowly vanishing vestiges of crumbling strata. Their destruction is a kind of creation, for what it accomplishes is the continuous revelation of new and hitherto hidden forms, even as a sculptor reveals the statue by chipping away the matrix that imprisons it. We can sense this never ending, two-edged process of destruction and creation even though we may not notice any significant changes during our time in the desert, or even during the span of our lives. Here, where the earth lies naked in the sun, free of any concealing mantle of soil or vegetation, the products of geomorphic process are so sharply delineated that they almost shout the stories of their continuing creation. And yet, though we seem to have just missed a stroke of the chisel, or about to witness the sculptor in action, seldom do we actually catch nature in the act of carving her creation. The landforms seem, rather, to stand in poses of arrested motion. When floods come, we may observe some cutting and carrying away of the soft, superficial materials by the same streams that deposited them, but the great rock foundations of the country reveal no signs of alteration. Only once, in Glen Canyon, have I seen anything but small pebbles dislodged from the great cliffs. On that single occasion, I looked up just as a giant slab of stone split away from the top of a sheer, thousand-foot wall of rock. For long seconds, it dropped silently in free fall. Then, hitting the top of the talus, it exploded into countless fragments, the thunder of its impact cannonading against the canyon walls.

Marble Gorge, from rim of Grand Canyon at Tatahatso Point

[*Willa Cather, in Death Comes for the Archbishop*]

One thing which struck [Father Latour] at once was that every mesa was duplicated by a cloud mesa, like a reflection, which lay motionless above it or moved slowly up from behind it. These cloud formations seemed to be always there, however hot and blue the sky. Sometimes they were flat terraces, ledges of vapour; sometimes they were dome-shaped, or fantastic, like the tops of silvery pagodas, rising one above another, as if an oriental city lay directly behind the rock. The great tables of granite set down in an empty plain were inconceivable without their attendant clouds, which were a part of them, as the smoke is part of the censer, or the foam of the wave.

Coming along the Santa Fe trail, in the vast plains of Kansas, Father Latour had found the sky more a desert than the land; a hard, empty blue, very monotonous to the eyes of a Frenchman. But west of the Pecos all that changed; here there was always activity overhead, clouds forming and moving all day long. Whether they were dark and full of violence, or soft and white with luxurious idleness, they powerfully affected the world beneath them. The desert, the mountains and mesas, were continually reformed and re-coloured by the cloud shadows. The whole country seemed fluid to the eye under this constant change of accent, this ever-varying distribution of light.

. . .

The weather alternated between blinding sand-storms and brilliant sunlight. The sky was as full of motion and change as the desert beneath it was monotonous and still —and there was so much sky, more than at sea, more than anywhere else in the world. The plain was there, under one's feet, but what one saw when one looked about was that brilliant blue world of stinging air and moving cloud. Even the mountains were mere ant-hills under it. Elsewhere the sky is the roof of the world; but here the earth was the floor of the sky. The landscape one longed for when one was far away, the thing all about one, the world one actually lived in, was the sky, the sky!

. . .

The voice that beautifies the land;
The voice above,
The voice of the thunder
Within the dark cloud
Again and again it sounds,
The voice that beautifies the land . . .
　　　　　—TWELFTH SONG OF THE THUNDER, MOUNTAINTOP WAY

When they left the rock or tree or sand dune that had sheltered them for the night, the Navajo was careful to obliterate every trace of their temporary occupation. He buried the embers of the fire and the remnants of food, unpiled any stones he had piled together, filled up the holes he had scooped in the sand. Since this was exactly Jacinto's procedure, Father Latour judged that, just as it was the white man's way to assert himself in any landscape, to change it, make it over a little (at least to leave some mark of memorial of his sojourn), it was the Indian's way to pass through a country without disturbing anything; to pass and leave no trace, like fish through the water, or birds through the air.

It was the Indian manner to vanish into the landscape, not to stand out against it. The Hopi villages that were set upon rock mesas were made to look like the rock on which they sat, were imperceptible at a distance. The Navajo hogans, among the sand and willows, were made of sand and willows. None of the pueblos would at that time admit glass windows into their dwellings. The reflection of the sun on the glazing was to them ugly and unnatural—even dangerous. Moreover, these Indians disliked novelty and change. They came and went by the old paths worn into the rock by the feet of their fathers, used the old natural stairway of stone to climb to their mesa towns, carried water from the old springs, even after white men had dug wells.

In the working of silver or drilling of turquoise the Indians had exhaustless patience; upon their blankets and belts and ceremonial robes they lavished their skill and pains. But their conception of decoration did not extend to the landscape. They seemed to have none of the European's desire to "master" nature, to arrange and re-create. They spent their ingenuity in the other direction; in accommodating themselves to the scene in which they found themselves. This was not so much from indolence, the Bishop thought, as from an inherited caution and respect. It was as if the great country were asleep, and they wished to carry on their lives without awakening it; or as if the spirits of earth and air and water were things not to antagonize and arouse. When they hunted, it was with the same discretion; an Indian hunt was never a slaughter. They ravaged neither the rivers nor the forest, and if they irrigated, they took as little water as would serve their needs. The land and all that it bore they treated with consideration; not attempting to improve it, they never desecrated it.

. . .

North of Laguna two Zuni runners sped by them, going somewhere east on "Indian business." They saluted Eusabio by gestures with the open palm, but did not stop. They coursed over the sand with the fleetness of young antelope, their bodies disappearing and reappearing among the sand dunes, like the shadows that eagles cast in their strong, unhurried flight. ◆

III. Variety

The earth is looking at me; it is looking up at me;
I, I am looking down at it.
I, I am happy, he is looking at me;
I, I am happy, I am looking at him.

The sun is looking at me; it is looking down at me;
I, I am looking up at it.
I, I am happy, it is looking at me;
I, I am happy, I am looking at it.

—Chant, When They Saw Each Other, Origin Legend

VARIETY is the outstanding fact of the Navajo Country. There is variety in the vegetation zones that mark elevation—spruce, fir, ponderosa, and aspen in the highlands, piñon, juniper, and sage at the middle altitudes, and grass grading into desert in the low country. There is variety in the landforms—plateaus, mesas, buttes, canyons, plains, and occasional mountains, with seemingly infinite variation on each theme. Gradually, if one has time to look long enough at Navajo Country, he becomes aware that distinct landscape styles can be recognized.

This sorting into styles is possible because of variations of rock type and of degree of erosion. If a featureless plain begins to be attacked by streams running across it, the erosion is at first downward. Running water and the tiny cutting-tools of silt and sand excavate trenchlike gashes in the flat surface, and canyon country is born. Down-cutting continues until the streams reach a level below which they cannot cut—perhaps the level of the region's master stream. Then the downward erosion becomes lateral, and the cliffs begin a slow but inexorable retreat from the streams that exposed them. The retreat is a ragged one, and some sections of the cliff recede faster than others, leaving behind outliers, the mesas and buttes that dot much of the Navajo Country. Finally, weathering and erosion reduce even these to sand and clay, and the land again becomes a plain, but a plain now lower by the thickness of the stratum that once rested upon it.

If the rock is hard, the forms that weather from it tend to be angular, with vertical cliffs exposed as the brittle rock breaks off in slabs, the break occurring through the thinnest dimension of the bed—across the layer. The weaker the rock is, the more susceptible it is to crumbling away, with a consequent rounding of corners and reduction of slope angle, and the more easily it can be attacked by even small, intermittent rivulets of water. The softest materials thus develop an extreme intricacy of drainage channels and form the kind of country we call badlands, where erosion is so rapid that almost no vegetation has time to take root.

Color is as variable as rock type and degree of erosion. Maroon-reds, brown-reds, red-oranges, yellow-oranges, lemon-yellows, and yellow-whites are all found in abundance, and bone-white, blue-gray, and pink are not infrequent. Volcanic basalts add black and chocolate-brown. Even greens are occasionally encountered.

The most variegated of all the rocks in the Navajo Country are those of the Chinle formation, which forms the brilliant badlands of the Painted Desert. The Paiute Indians, a few of whom live on the Navajo Reservation, call these bright, banded clays "rainbow-lying-down."

In Beautiful Valley, southwest of Canyon de Chelly, Painted Desert landscapes have been eroded into red and gray clays, and logs of yellow and red petrified wood, said to be the bones of Big Monster, lie scattered about. In some places, the chips of agatized wood lie so thickly that the ground is paved with them. It is difficult to visualize this land as it was when the Chinle formation was being laid down. Great swamps then covered the country; there was luxuriant vegetation everywhere, and dinosaurs and

Aspens and pine near Buffalo Pass, Chuska Mountains

other strange reptiles wandered about. Today, bare, gray bentonites form rounded mounds that stretch away in a scene of incredibly austere sterility.

Some miles west of Canyon de Chelly is another superb area of badlands, but of a character entirely different from that of Beautiful Valley. This is Salina (Tselani) Breaks, where soft sandstones of yellow and off-white have been carved into an amazing variety of spires, sharp fins, seamed ridges, and pedestal rocks. Some of the formations found at Tselani also occur many miles to the southwest in the badlands of the Coal Canyon system, but in this territory the rocks are multicolored, and the forms are even more varied and bizarre. Incredible pinnacles, pedestals, spires, and balanced rocks line many of these canyons, while in other tributaries, scalloped but otherwise relatively smooth walls are striped with broad bands of red and white.

Outside the canyon complexes there are vast open stretches of the Navajo Country with a wonderful feeling of space and freedom. I like best the drive from the pine forests at the foot of the San Francisco Peaks eastward to the Hopi Buttes. Beyond the woodlands and past the last

of the reddish black cinder cones of the San Francisco Volcanic Field stretches a vast panorama. The broad, valley of the Little Colorado, dappled by cloud shadows, is in the foreground, and beyond a plain extends to the distant blue bumps on the horizon that are the Hopi Buttes. Crossing the sometimes dry river at Leupp, the road proceeds across the open plain. The immense sky and the endless procession of white, cottony clouds are enough to maintain your exhilaration as you bounce along over rutted dirt and through sand, leaving a wake of swirling dust.

The buttes loom larger and larger on the horizon, their blue peaks rising up, as the early geologist John Newberry described them, "like ships approached at sea—some in cones and symmetrical castellated slopes and others in irregular masses," until at last you are opposite the scored sides of Elephant Butte. Ahead is an array of buttes—Castle Butte, French Butte, Chimney Butte, Pumpkin Flower, each unique and outstanding, yet each a variation on the common theme of black volcanic rock rimmed at the base by eroded, red, fine-grained deposits.

He has a voice, he has a voice.
Just at daylight the Mountain Bluebird calls.
The blue bird has a voice,
He has a voice, his voice melodious,
His voice melodious, that flows in gladness.
The bluebird calls, the bluebird calls.
                              —DAYLIGHT SONG

Yucca and daisies, Bridge Canyon

[65

IV. Mountain and Plain

From meadows green where ponds are scattered,
From there we come.
Bereft of limbs, one bears another,
From there we come.
Bereft of eyes, one bears another,
From there we come.
By ponds where healing herbs are growing,
From there we come.
With these your limbs you shall recover.
From there we come.
With these your eyes you shall recover.
From there we come.
—Song of the Stricken Twins, Night Way Myth

IN A LAND of little rain, the Chuska Mountains, which bisect the Navajo Country, are something of a surprise. Their altitude makes them different; it has allowed for fragrant forests, duck-dotted lakes, meadows and marshes. Virgin groves of ponderosa pine are interspersed with aspen thickets and well-grazed grassy parks, and countless depressions hold seasonal lakes and an occasional permanent one. In the cool canyons on the mountains' western slope streams are bordered by spruce, fir, and flowers that one would expect a thousand miles farther north. The cool, well-watered environment of the Chuska Range provides an island in the desert for the life forms that require it.

Along the east side of the range stretches an abrupt sandstone scarp that gives an unobstructed view across the great San Juan Basin. On clear days it is possible to see a hundred and fifty miles or more to the north, where the needle-like spire of Lizard Head Peak marks the La Plata and San Juan Mountains in Colorado. Camp in one of the small grassy spaces on the edge of the scarp east of Deadman Lake and observe the many moods of weather over the basin. It is almost like having a cloud of your own for an observation post.

Usually the basin looks dry and brown, in startling contrast to the mountaintop. Dust devils dance in the far distance, and haze hangs in the air. Sometimes, though only rarely, a great storm half-drowns the basin. Then,

from the mountain, the land seems to shine with wetness, and brimming ponds and charcos dot its surface, glinting in the sun. Forgotten rivers run again, muddy and wild and full of balls of tumbleweed flushed from the drifts of brush that have blown into sand-choked channels for the many dry days between rains.

One night, driving along at sixty miles an hour on the basin floor, I suddenly came to a dip in the highway, across which was running a wash in full flood, though it had not rained in the immediate vicinity. Not having time even to slow down, I plowed into the rushing water. For a few exciting seconds, nothing was visible through the windshield but a yellow wall of water illuminated by my headlights. My momentum was enough to carry me across the wash, but I continued on my way with added respect for nature's surprises and her power in this country, even on the paved highway.

Descending from the crest of the Chuskas toward the basin, one passes through dissected foothills clothed in juniper and piñon pine. In some places only a sparse cover of grass and weeds half-hides the yellow-gray, stone-dotted clay between the trees. Elsewhere, sagebrush and greasewood fill the gaps. When rain wets sage and juniper, their fragrances mingle beautifully. On the flats at the foot of the mountains all trees are left behind. Scattered shrubs and an occasional tuft of grass try vainly to hold the sandy soil together, but they succeed only in clinging to a few

grains around the roots and are left sitting on pedestals as the wind whips away the rest of the soil, to drift it up in low dunes somewhere farther on.

A discontinuous band of badlands stretches in a northeast-southwest direction across the plains of the San Juan Basin. In places, the barren, sharp-crested, steeply sloping ridges of clay are striped in shades of gray and ochre on a tan and bone-white base. In other spots, such as near Bistai, a peculiar brick-red, clinkerlike formation outcrops, along with charcoal-colored clays, giving the country the look of a burned-out hell. It was scenes like these that inspired Lt. James Simpson, in 1849, to describe the soil as "... presenting very much the levity and color of ashes and looking, if possible, more under a *curse* than the generality of that we have passed over." In contrast, some of the higher parts of the basin have abundant grass, despite heavy grazing; and the few mesas of the region sometimes support growths of piñon or even ponderosa.

The basin is cut across its middle by the shallow canyon of the Chaco, a dry river that eventually reaches the San Juan above Shiprock. Here, nine hundred years ago, was the center of the plateau country's greatest prehistoric civilization, that of the Anasazi, the "Ancient Enemies" of the Navajo. The Anasazi were a Pueblo people, and their descendants still dwell in the terraced apartment houses of Zuni, Acoma, the Hopi Country and the Rio Grande, but in and around Chaco Canyon are the most elaborate remains of their golden age: great pueblos of stone, giant circular ceremonial structures and tall tower kivas, built with the finest prehistoric masonry north of central Mexico.

The finest of the ruins is Pueblo Bonito. A great D-shaped dwelling, its scores of square rooms and circular ceremonial kivas seem a giant honeycomb from the canyon rim above. Some of the walls of the pueblo still stand three stories tall, and much of the masonry is exquisite. In places, courses of shaped, brick-sized stones alternate with a series of much smaller stones to make an eye-pleasing mosaic. In one part of the ruins, five successive rooms are visible through a series of doorways, and variations in the light admitted to the rooms impart to the stones of each a different shade of yellow-brown.

For a few centuries Pueblo Bonito was the center of the flowering of a unique and creative culture, a center from which ideas and art radiated to the entire Southwest and to which trade goods from Mexico—parrots and copper bells—found their way. Traders haggled in the houses, masked dancers emerged from subterranean kivas, and children played in the plaza.

Then the people vanished, and for nine centuries the windows of the crumbling dwellings stared vacantly across the desert. Now only the daytime sees a momentary return of human life, as infrequent visitors enter, ponder, and depart. With nightfall, the stones return again to the silent possession of the spiders, the scorpions, and the *chindi*—ghosts of the dead.

Far up above me, a thousand feet or so, set in a great cavern in the face of the cliff, I saw a little city of stone asleep. It was as still as sculpture—and something like that. It all hung together, seemed to have a kind of composition: pale little houses of stone nestling close to one another, perched on top of each other, with flat roofs, narrow windows, straight walls, and in the middle of the group, a round tower.

In sunlight it was the colour of winter oak leaves. A fringe of cedars grew along the edge of the cavern, like a garden. They were the only living things. Such silence and stillness and repose—immortal repose. That village sat looking down into the canyon with the calmness of eternity...I had come upon the city of some extinct civilization, hidden away in this inaccessible mesa for centuries, preserved in the dry air and almost perpetual sunlight like a fly in amber, guarded by the cliffs and the river and the desert.

—WILLA CATHER

Mummy Cave Ruin, Canyon de Chelly

[*Willa Cather, The Song of the Lark*]

The Cliff-Dwellers liked wide cañons, where the great cliffs caught
the sun. Panther Cañon had been deserted for hundreds of years when the
first Spanish missionaries came into Arizona, but the masonry of the
houses was still wonderfully firm; had crumbled only where a landslide
or a rolling boulder had torn it.

All the houses in the cañon were clean with the cleanness of
sun-baked, wind-swept places, and they all smelled of the tough little
cedars that twisted themselves into the very doorways. One of these
rock-rooms Thea took for her own.

. . .

Antelope House Ruin, Canyon del Muerto

Thea went down to the stream by the Indian water-trail. She had found a bathing-pool with a sand bottom, where the creek was dammed by fallen trees. The climb back was long and steep, and when she reached her little house in the cliff, she always felt fresh delight in its comfort and inaccessibility. By the time she got there, the woolly red-and-grey blankets were saturated with sunlight, and she sometimes fell asleep as soon as she stretched her body on their warm surfaces. She used to wonder at her own inactivity. She could lie there hour after hour in the sun and listen to the strident whirr of the big locusts, and to the light, ironical laughter of the quaking aspens. All her life she had been hurrying and sputtering, as if she had been born behind time and had been trying to catch up. Now, she reflected, as she drew herself out long upon the rugs, it was as if she were waiting for something to catch up with her. She had got to a place where she was out of the stream of meaningless activity and undirected effort.

Here she could lie for half a day undistracted, holding pleasant and incomplete conceptions in her mind—almost in her hands. They were scarcely clear enough to be called ideas. They had something to do with fragrance and colour and sound, but almost nothing to do with words.

. . .

And now her power to think seemed converted into a power of sustained sensation. She could become a mere receptacle for heat, or become a colour, like the bright lizards that darted about on the hot stones outside her door; or she could become a continuous repetition of sound, like the cicadas.

. . .

Shale at base of Vermillion Cliffs, near Lee's Ferry

Panther Cañon was the home of innumerable swallows. They built nests in the wall far above the hollow groove in which Thea's own rock-chamber lay. They seldom ventured above the rim of the cañon, to the flat, wind-swept tableland. Their world was the blue air-river between the cañon walls. In that blue gulf the arrow-shaped birds swam all day long, with only an occasional movement of the wings. The only sad thing about them was their timidity: the way in which they lived their lives between the echoing cliffs and never dared to rise out of the shadow of the cañon walls. As they swam past her door, Thea often felt how easy it would be to dream one's life out in some cleft in the world.

From the ancient dwelling there came always a dignified, unobtrusive sadness; now stronger, now fainter—like the aromatic smell which the dwarf cedars gave out in the sun—but always present, a part of the air one breathed. At night, when Thea dreamed about the cañon— or in the early morning when she hurried toward it, anticipating it— her conception of it was of yellow rocks baking in sunlight, the swallows, the cedar smell, and that peculiar sadness—a voice out of the past, not very loud, that went on saying a few simple things to the solitude eternally.

. . .

Mummy Cave Ruin, Canyon del Muerto

It seemed to Thea that a certain understanding of those old people came up to her out of the rockshelf on which she lay; that certain feelings were transmitted to her, suggestions that were simple, insistent, and monotonous, like the beating of Indian drums. They were not expressible in words, but seemed rather to translate themselves into attitudes of body, into degrees of muscular tension or relaxation; the naked strength of youth, sharp as the sun-shafts; the crouching timorousness of age, the sullenness of women who waited for their captors.

· · ·

Pueblo Bonito, Chaco Canyon National Monument

. . . all their customs and ceremonies and their religion went back to water. The men provided the food, but water was the care of the women. The stupid women carried water for most of their lives; the cleverer ones made the vessels to hold it. Their pottery was their most direct appeal to water, the envelope and sheath of the precious element itself. The strongest Indian need was expressed in those graceful jars, fashioned slowly by hand, without the aid of a wheel.

When Thea took her bath at the bottom of the cañon, in the sunny pool behind the screen of cottonwoods, she sometimes felt as if the water must have sovereign qualities, from having been the object of so much service and desire. That stream was the only living thing left of the drama that had been played out in the cañon centuries ago. In the rapid, restless heart of it, flowing swifter than the rest, there was a continuity of life that reached back into the old time. The glittering thread of current had a kind of lightly worn, loosely knit personality, graceful and laughing. Thea's bath came to have a ceremonial gravity. The atmosphere of the cañon was ritualistic. ◆

V. Anasazi

THE ANASAZI cities are not the kind of constructions that intrude on the natural scene, for they were built of the same materials the land was —stone and mud—and their blocky and terraced forms echo those of the cliffs and talus surrounding them.

Some ruins, of villages built in the open on mesa tops or in valleys, have crumbled to piles of rubble whose outlines only vaguely suggest their original forms, and only the decorated potsherds scattered about remain as evidence of the builders' artistry. Other pueblos, better built, have lasted longer. In places, as at Chaco Canyon, some walls still stand three stories high. None of these open sites, however, can compare for romantic appeal to the cliff dwellings hidden in the countless caves that are shallowly excavated into the sandstone canyon walls. How much more exciting it is to explore a canyon with the knowledge that the next cave may contain a cliff city or, at least, an ancient house or storage structure.

Another hoped-for, yet somehow always unexpected, event is the discovery of prehistoric drawings on the rocks. Petroglyphs—pecked into the rock—and painted pictographs of amazing variety, dating from eras of great antiquity to the present day, occur throughout the region. Bighorn sheep, hunters, fluteplayers, dancers—these are some of the common themes, and there are a variety of geometric designs, hand prints, and seemingly aimless squiggles. The motivation for these drawings remains a mystery, although we may suppose that both religious and aesthetic considerations were important.

One of the great concentrations of prehistoric remains in the Southwest is in the Tsegi Canyon system, center of the Kayenta branch of the Anasazi. The two most important of the ruins, Betatakin and Keet Seel, are protected by Navajo National Monument. In addition, several other major sites are found in the canyons, notable among which are Bat Woman House and Twin Caves Ruin in Dowozhibito Canyon.

The most wonderful ruin in the Southwest is Betatakin, in a canyon tributary to Tsegi. Here, in an enormous hemispherical cave, lies an extremely well-preserved ruin of some one hundred and twenty rooms. In late afternoon, when the sunlight reflected off the canyon walls imparts a warm orange glow to the whole vaulted cavern, the com-bination of light, color, and antiquity creates an atmosphere more magic than that of any other ruin.

Keet Seel, however, surpasses even Betatakin in giving an idea of 13th century life in these canyons. Reached by foot or on the back of a ragged-gaited Navajo horse, Keet Seel stands in the remote upper reaches of a canyon tributary. The trail to the ruin wends its way along the bottom of the fifty-foot deep, steep-sided arroyo that has been cut into the alluvium lying along the canyon bottom. One feels hemmed in by the walls of sediment and disappointed at not being able to enjoy the canyon's red cliffs and tree-filled coves, sight of them cut off by the high banks of the arroyo. Though not all the work of the arroyo has been destructive of beauty—the channel-trenching has exhumed several buried waterfalls formed by ledges in the canyon's rock foundation—still one cannot help but consider, if he knows the story of the canyons, what a beautiful, verdant place the Tsegi must have been before 1884, when unusually heavy rains and the destruction by overgrazing of much of the plant cover led to great floods and the cutting of the deep arroyos that now snake up the canyon and its many tributaries. Before that time, the waters of the creek spread out over the canyon bottom at flood time, unconfined by the narrow arroyo, depositing sediment rather than eroding it. Marshes and lakes lay in the hollows and swales of the poorly defined channel, and wildlife frequented these oases. With the cutting of the arroyo, the lakes were drained, floods no longer spread out to water the lush grasses, and the scarred former flood plain became a semidesert supporting cactus and yucca instead of grass and reeds. Today the only evidence of the Tsegi's lush past is the black, lacustrian sediments that are visible in the arroyo walls, and in the now meaningless names Laguna Creek and Marsh Pass.

Arroyo-cutting is not a story of Tsegi Canyon only. All over the Southwest the same process took place in one drainage after another. Near Fort Defiance, on the Navajo Reservation, Lt. James Simpson observed in 1849 that his party had a pleasant camping place, "a small pond or lake, bordered by a margin of green luxurient grass, being directly in front of us to gladen our sight . . . some ducks, I notice, are constantly hovering over this spot." Overgrazing led to the destruction of the vegetative cover, and

during the early 1880's channel trenching began. Today the lake is gone, the ducks are gone, and the luxuriant grass is gone, replaced by the scar of an arroyo. The destruction of the Navajo's land by the overgrazing of Navajo flocks adds new irony to "as long as the grass shall grow."

Perhaps overgrazing cannot be assigned the entire blame for this kind of erosion; there is ample evidence that arroyo-cutting occurred in the past, long before domesticated animals were present, but never during the occupation of the pre-nineteenth-century Navajos nor that of their Puebloan predecessors was there channel-trenching of such extent and magnitude. Sheep overpopulation has undoubtedly contributed not only to the destruction of the grass but also, through nature's inevitable interrelations, to the destruction of the soil and depletion of the water supplies on which the grass depended. Like the ripples on the pebble-broken surface of a pond, the destruction of one part in the equilibrium of an ecosystem is felt as an ever expanding wave of change until a new, and often less desirable kind of balance is achieved.

After a dozen miles of trail, Keet Seel is reached. The ruin lies on a gigantic overhung ledge that faces green cottonwoods and red cliffs. A ladder must be climbed to gain the shelf along which the cave city stretches for three hundred and fifty feet. The ruin—if that is the proper word for such a well-preserved village—contains about one hundred and sixty rooms, most of which look as though they had been built only a few months ago, not seven centuries. From the beams of the log and pole ceilings hang the little loops of yucca fiber from which the ancients suspended their possessions. Tiny corn cobs and bits of squash rind are scattered about and lie piled in bins, and milling stones sit in troughlike metates as if waiting for their owners to return to the daily task of corn-grinding. At one spot archaeologists have left a cooking pot of corrugated ware as an example of the pottery that was found in the ruin when it was first investigated.

Sitting in the shaded cave among the ancient houses, surrounded by silence, one's subconscious strains to hear the sounds of life: the voices of women gossiping in confidential tones over their metates, glancing around now and again with ill-suppressed giggles; the laughter of dark-eyed children; or even the yapping of a dog. But the cave remains silent, and the wonder of the deserted village returns with added poignancy. Where went the people who built this place and breathed life into it? Why, after living here only a few decades, did they leave, never to return?

Small round holes that can be seen in some of the beams projecting from the housetops have revealed what some believe to be the answer. Here and there a dendro-

chronologist has removed cores of wood to date the ruin and to tell something about conditions of climate during its occupation. This he does by examining the tree's annual growth rings, the variation in width reflecting year-to-year differences in precipitation and temperature. The study of these and other ancient logs has shown that during the period of abandonment of the latest of these ruins a deficiency of moisture occurred in the early summer growth season, and this observation has led to the great-drought theory of pueblo abandonment. A good theory, except that archaeology indicates that the Tsegi or Kayenta people moved to less well-watered lands to the south in the Hopi country and the valley of the Little Colorado, hardly expectable behavior for a drought-driven people.

A more sophisticated theory has been suggested from evidence of an ancient arroyo revealed by the cutting of the present one. The sediments and the datable potsherds contained therein indicate that excavation of an arroyo which was later filled in again took place some time after A.D. 1150-1200 and before the mid-nineteenth century, suggesting the possibility that during the late Anasazi occupation of the Tsegi, channel-trenching caused flood waters to be concentrated in narrow, steep-sided arroyos, thus preventing the overflow of water onto the flood plain. Without this overflow available for crops planted there, cultivation might no longer have been possible.

Although this could have happened in Tsegi canyon and might have caused abandonment, we don't know that it did; the dating of the fossil arroyo is imprecise, and we do not know to what extent farming here relied on flood-water. We know that arroyo-cutting was not a significant factor at certain other Anasazi centers, such as Mesa Verde, which were abandoned at about the same time.

The Tsegi Country is now inhabited by Navajos, who long engaged in raiding the earlier residents, and some scholars have suggested that the ancient Anasazi were displaced by the warlike Navajos and their linguistic relatives, the Apache. Many of the pueblos of the period in question are built in almost inaccessible caves or on steep-sided mesas and show signs of having been constructed with defense in mind. However, not all structures of this period were defensible, and in the Tsegi, the vital water supplies do not appear to have been fortified. The evidence that the Navajos and the Apaches were in this region early enough to have caused these abandonments is doubtful at best. Thus these and other theories attempting to explain the desertion of the great pueblos and cliff dwellings are each weakened by serious drawbacks, and the question remains unanswered.

From the flat red sea of sand rose great rock mesas, generally Gothic in outline, resembling vast cathedrals. They were not crowded together in disorder, but placed in wide spaces, long vistas between. This plain might once have been an enormous city, all the smaller quarters destroyed by time, only the public buildings left . . .

This mesa plain had an appearance of great antiquity, and of incompleteness; as if, with all the materials for world-making assembled, the Creator had desisted, gone away and left everything on the point of being brought together, on the eve of being arranged into mountain, plain, plateau. The country was still waiting to be made into a landscape.

—WILLA CATHER

VI. Buttes, Mesas, Monuments

THERE IS something about a landscape of dramatic buttes and mesas and monuments that has a fascination beyond that of simple aesthetics. Part of this fascination is due to the apparent improbability of the forms. Many men of many cultures have found such configurations appealing. Romanticist landscape paintings, both in the western world and in the orient, often emphasize strangeness of shape. A Chinese guidebook to a famous mountain states that, "unless a mountain has strange peaks and curious rocks to shape its scenic beauty . . . it will not claim the attention of generations of people." But beyond this, beyond drama and improbability, buttes and mesas have an intriguing architectural quality. Despite a knowledge of the natural processes that create these flat-topped, vertical-sided landforms, despite the realization that horizontal rock layers in an arid land inevitably yield sheer-sided, angular forms when carved by flood and sand, our inner minds resist and strive to see in mesas and monuments a conscious hand guiding the processes of landscape sculpture. It is this juxtaposition of the seemingly planned on what we nevertheless know to be natural that elicits our wonder.

In the northwestern portion of the San Juan Basin is a landscape that brings to mind the surface of the moon. Buttes of sandstone on bases of bluish gray clay stand as stark outliers of Mesa Verde, and far to the south fantastic stone pinnacles and mesas rise above the plain. Across the San Juan River looms the double-spired form of Shiprock, its dark, fluted mass appearing to float on a grassy sea. The Navajos call it Winged Rock, believing it to be the petrified remains of the eagle-like Rock Monster of legend. It is also said to be an arrow guarding the recumbent figure of the Carrizo Mountains. From the pinnacle's south and west sides radiate two wall-like dikes of dark volcanic rock—remains, like Shiprock itself, of ancient igneous activity, the roots of a volcano long since

eroded away along with the rock layer on which it rested. These dikes are the congealed blood of Rock Monster, say the Navajos.

To the southward are other moonscapes. Table Mesa rises abruptly, its cliffs resting on eroded blue-gray shales. Smaller mesas flank it, as do the vertically scored sides of volcanic Akeah Peak. Off to the east rises the knifelike ridge of Hogback Mountain; and farther to the south stand craggy Bennet Peak and its smaller companion, Ford Butte—both of volcanic origin.

Not many miles west of Shiprock, between the Lukachukai Mountain section of the Chuskas and the laccolithic Carrizo Mountains to the north, lies an almost unknown region of buttes, natural arches, canyons, and ruins. This is the red rock country, a rugged land carved from red-orange Wingate sandstone. Here the Wingate forms smooth, alcove-indented cliffs and square-shouldered buttes and mesas. In Redrock Valley fantastic spires have been left by retreating cliffs, and half a dozen or more natural windows have been eroded into spurs and fins of fiery sandstone. The greatest of these windows is the Gothic-style opening known as Royal Arch, which rivals Rainbow Bridge in height.

In addition to its natural features, the red rock country has a number of ancient cliff dwellings hidden in its canyons, and this has given rise to legends of lost Anasazi cities. In Hasbidibito Valley is the three-story Rotten Rock Ruin, and also Painted Cave, where some of the Navajo country's most colorful pictographs have been daubed onto the rock walls of a ruin-sheltering cave. Human figures with headdresses are done in red, white, bluegreen, and yellow mineral paint. There are dozens of handprints and geometric designs. Many of these paintings appear to date from the days of the Basketmakers, pre-Puebloan ancestors of the Anasazi.

This Wingate sandstone country is continued to the southwest by the impressive cathedral-like form of Round Rock and by the discontinuous cliffs of Ventana Mesa, with their numerous natural arches and windows, the best of them the delicate inverted teardrop opening of Hope Arch. All this region of red rock is, however, only a prelude to the best of all butte and mesa country, the stone

symphony of Monument Valley. Words like "grand" and "magnificent" paint but pale pictures of the impact of this great city of stone.

City of stone. It is difficult to escape the comparison between the great monoliths of the Valley and a city of skyscrapers. John Newberry, first geologist to traverse the region (1859), was unable to escape it: ". . . scattered over the interval are many castle-like buttes and slender towers, none of which can be less than 1,000 feet in height, their sides absolutely perpendicular, their forms wonderful imitations of the structures of human art . . . we could hardly resist the conviction that we beheld the walls and towers of some Cyclopean city hitherto undiscovered in this faroff region."

If the buttes of Monument Valley are masterpieces of architecture, then East Mitten is a good example of the sculptor's skill. Its fissured form is different from every new viewpoint, yet it remains a compact, harmonious whole. But the most amazing thing about the Valley is not the beauty of the individual monuments, remarkable as they are, nor the sheer improbability of some of the slim, soaring shafts and pedestal rocks. It is the arrangement of these forms into a balanced, integrated composition in space that is astounding. Wherever one moves among the monuments, the ever-changing vista of buttes and mesas always makes a supremely pleasing panorama. It strains credulity to consider that this placement of the monuments was undirected save by unconscious laws of nature.

The Navajo Country, and particularly Monument Valley, is a land of the magnificent and monumental; it is not an intimate landscape for the most part. Yet tucked away in the folds of the mesa behind the great monuments is an area of delicate natural arches and tiny cliff dwellings in perfect contrast to the almost overwhelming grandeur of the monuments. Some of the finest of these are in Tse Bighi, "Within the Rocks," just behind the monuments. Here is Moccasin Arch and Ear of the Wind Arch, and the aperture known as the Sun's Eye, complete with eyelash-like streaks on the rock; here also the alcove called the Big Hogan because of its dome-like interior and circular "smoke hole"; and here neatly pecked petroglyphs of bighorn sheep, turkeys, and hunters; and the

two round prehistoric structures in the resonating chamber of Echo Cave. But the best collection of such gems is on the other side of the mesa, in Mystery Valley. Here are a dozen or more natural arches—some of them double—and numerous tiny cliff dwellings and storage structures. Under the south buttress of Wedding Ring Arch are two stone and adobe rooms, called the Honeymoon Cottage. In one spot, a cave containing the foundations of a ruin is connected by an opening in its side to the arched-over outlet of two perfectly round, now dry plunge pools, an arrangement that must once have been very satisfactory to the cave's occupants.

I remember one small ruin in Mystery Valley particularly well. It was one I had heard about but had not seen on my previous visit to the Valley. I approached it just at sunset, walking across the rounded slickrock top of a spur of the mesa, and as I reached the rim of a tiny canyon and looked down at the double-walled ruin in its cave, the fiery day-end glow unique to Monument Valley lit everything, rock and ruin alike, as if it were in the heart of a furnace.

Another time I came to Mystery Valley looking for a small ruin mentioned in an early archaeological report. I knew I was in the right area but couldn't find the exact spot. Then I noticed sherds of pottery in the sandy bottom of a small dry wash. I followed these up what had been the stream until they abruptly disappeared opposite a sand-filled cave. A few seconds digging in the dune revealed a corner of the "missing" ruin, which had been completely buried by wind-blown sand during the previous half-century.

There are other corners of Monument Valley equally enticing. There are the odd monuments of thin-bedded orange-brown stone in Copper Canyon. There is Comb Ridge, with its weird rock formations, minor ruins, and an arch or two. The great cliff dwelling known as Poncho House lies just outside Monument Valley, as do several smaller ruins. Perhaps the greatest experience of all, though, is ascending Hunts Mesa and looking out across the monuments from the Rim, where one has a full view of one of the great scenic treasure houses of the world.

It has often been remarked that the colors and the character of Monument Valley are constantly changing, are never the same from one moment to the next. Common as this observation is, it must be repeated here, for this change is inseparable from the personality of the Valley.

At dawn, the shapes of the monuments are drawn in black against a pale yellow sky. Gradually the sun brushes the monument tops with gold, and the forms of their ruddy lower cliffs become visible in the diffuse, indirect light. As the sun climbs higher, it warms both the air and the color of the stone. The sun is still low enough to graze the sides of the monuments, and it makes shadows where crevices crease the faces of the cliffs.

Later, at midday when the sun is overhead, the forms and colors go flat; crisp, black shadows disappear and are replaced by a few bluish streaks. Dust begins to blow about, and the moisture in the air now becomes manifest in puffs of cumulus cloud. By late afternoon, storms may be moving across the Valley, some whose gray wisps of rain evaporate before reaching the ground, others whose violent torrents of lightning-accompanied rain start muddy walls of water tumbling down steep-sided arroyos and send waterfalls leaping from glistening cliff tops.

The setting sun brings an entirely different mood to the Valley. In the evening the monuments begin to become orange again, but they soon surpass the merely warm aura of the morning. They begin to glow with a light that seems to radiate from within the stone itself, an incandescence that increases until it seems the red-hot rock must founder, and flow like molten metal. Then, in a very short space of time, the color cools through red-purple to a gentle violet edged with indigo, and the mile-long shadows of the monuments merge with the dark as it enters the Valley and gradually engulfs it.

Evening light on West Mitten Butte, Monument Valley

VII. Canyon de Chelly

THE MONUMENTS of Monument Valley are mostly made of De Chelly sandstone. The place from which this rock takes its name is Canyon de Chelly, its Spanish name a corruption of the Navajo *tseghi*, which means "rock canyon." This canyon and its major tributary, Canyon del Muerto, were cut into the humpbacked Defiance Uplift by streams originating in the Chuska Mountains. The canyon walls are often sheer or even overhanging and vary in color from pinkish through orange to purple-brown. In some places, they are smooth and uniform in color for five hundred vertical feet or more; in other places, ledges, overhangs, cracks, or crossbedding interrupt the otherwise even flow of the rock forms. The cross-bedding, remains of ancient sand dunes, often weathers into contorted curves and swirls, with thin, etched, parallel beds sweeping upward to an abrupt termination against another series of beds laid at right angles. In the late afternoon light, when the canyons take on something of the fire that burns brightest in Monument Valley, these waves of lined rock look like something from the Inferno.

Although they share a distinctive sculptural style, each of the major canyons has its own character. De Chelly is the more monumental of the two, but its companion canyon, del Muerto, is gentler and more intimate. As he ascends del Muerto the visitor passes through groves of cottonwoods, past peach orchards, and alongside Indian cornfields, all dominated by the sheer, towering, red-orange walls. Between either rim of the canyon is a strip of brilliant blue sky punctuated by puffy white clouds.

I think my favorite place in the canyon is where it meets Twin Trail Canyon. Here the green grass is at its tallest and the cornfields are most extensive. The canyon widens as two side canyons join it and makes a broad, sky-vaulted, cliff-rimmed valley. Like traditional southwestern Indian jewelry, with its red coral, green and blue turquoise, and white shell, the scene is a mosaic of clear colors and well-defined forms.

Canyon de Chelly's natural beauty would be enough to establish it as one of the West's major landmarks, yet the canyons also contain one of the largest concentrations of cliff dwellings in the Southwest. Huddling under sheltering cliffs, clinging to the sloping floors of caves, and nestled on seemingly inaccessible ledges of the canyon walls are scores of dwellings, both great and small. Little wonder that the Navajos call the vanished cliff dwellers the Swallow People, likening them to cliff swallows, who build their adobe nests under rocky canyon ledges.

Perhaps the most beautiful of the ruins is White House, in de Chelly. Set in a deep slot some fifty feet above the canyon floor, this sizable but compact dwelling is dwarfed by the smooth cliff that sweeps hundreds of feet skyward above it. Antelope House, in del Muerto, is a large but rather unlovely ruin at the base of a cliff. Up canyon is Standing Cow Ruin. The architectural remains here are minimal, but this is the site of some of the best pictographs in the canyon system's unparalleled collection, which ranges in period from Basketmaker to modern Navajo. The shallow cave in which Standing Cow Ruin is located is used by a nearby Navajo family as a storage room for dried peaches and other items, and a loom stands in the shade here. Perhaps it was an ancestor of these Navajos who painted the large, beautifully executed gray and white cow that gives the ruin its name. The large cow and its smaller companion are not the only pictographs at this site. Along a ledge above and to the left of the cave is the most remarkable Navajo pictograph panel extant, the Spanish Expedition Mural. Here are over a dozen separate

figures thought to portray an early expedition of Spaniards. Mounted men, wearing hats and carrying guns, ride across the cliff from left to right. Though most of the pictured Spaniards are clothed in white, one wears a russet brown robe marked with a white cross. In the background, is a pinto pony, and on it what is apparently an Indian with lance, shield, and feathered headdress.

The Expedition Mural tells only a part of the dramatic history of Canyon de Chelly. Inhabited at various times by the Basketmakers, cliff dwellers, Hopi Indians and Navajos, its canyons have experienced moments of violence as well as long peaceful periods. In 1805, many Navajo women and children were slaughtered by Spaniards in Massacre Cave high on the north wall of Canyon del Muerto, and in 1864 Kit Carson's troops, destroying sheep and fields as they went, systematically rounded up most of the Navajos, many of whom had retreated to almost unscalable rocks in the canyons for a last stand. Deprived of food, they were forced to surrender and to submit to the Long Walk into exile at Fort Sumner, New Mexico, from where they returned four years later after the failure of the reservation experiment.

The Canyon de Chelly system occupies a special place in Navajo folklore as well as in Navajo history. Many of the canyon's features have myths attached—Spider Rock, for example. Spider Rock is a spire that rises eight hundred feet from the canyon floor yet still falls two hundred feet short of the rim. Atop this rock is the legendary home of Spider Woman, who according to myth taught weaving to the Navajos.

I have seen Spider Rock many times, from the canyon rim and from the canyon floor. I have seen it in the morning, in the middle of the day and in the last hours of daylight, its sun-burnished shaft glowing against velvet-black background of shadow. But no view will ever equal the one of a certain late summer afternoon. We were getting ready for dinner at our camp some distance from the rim. An afternoon storm was passing overhead and sprinkling us with a light rain. Looking up, we suddenly realized that a rainbow was forming. Without a word, we ran through the junipers to the canyon rim. There, bathed in a pale violet light, was Spider Rock, and arching over the spire as well as plunging vertically into the depths of the canyon was a three-quarter circle double rainbow.

In the house of long life, there I wander.
In the house of happiness, there I wander.
Beauty before me, with it I wander.
Beauty behind me, with it I wander.
Beauty below me, with it I wander.
Beauty above me, with it I wander.
Beauty all around me, with it I wander.
In old age traveling, with it I wander.
On the beautiful trail I am, with it I wander.
—DAWN BOY'S SONG ON ENTERING WHITE HOUSE

Stormlight at mouth of Canyon de Chelly

At first light, before dawn, the desert is intimate, and each man feels the presence of others as an intrusion. Blinding colour has not supplanted soft greys, uncertain forms; cliffs harsh by daylight, and thunderous-walled cañons loom soft with wells of coolness. The east is white — mother-of-pearl — the world is secret to each one's self.

—Oliver La Farge

The great pines stand at a considerable distance from each other. Each tree grows alone, murmurs alone, thinks alone. They so not intrude upon each other. The Navajos are not much in the habit of giving or of asking help. Their language is not a communicative one, and they never attempt an interchange of personality in speech. Over their forests there is the same inexorable reserve. Each tree has its exalted power to bear.

—WILLA CATHER

Juniper, west side of Redbud Pass

Dewdrops and pollens may I enjoy.
With these may it be beautiful in front of me.
With these may it be beautiful behind me . . .
All is beautiful again. All is restored in beauty.
— MALE SHOOTING WAY

VIII. Wildlands of the Northwest

It increases and spreads
In the middle of the wide field
The white corn, it increases and spreads
Good and everlasting one, it increases and spreads.
—NAVAJO GROWTH SONG

EACH OF THE varied landscapes of the Navajo Country has its particular appeal to one who seeks spectacular or unusual beauty. But it is the great roadless northwestern part of the Reservation—an incredibly vast and rugged land of canyon and mesa, slickrock and sand—that calls to the lover of wilderness.

Much of this wild area is drained by the Navajo Canyon system. Though the magnificent lower end of Navajo Canyon has all but vanished beneath Lake Powell, its tributaries have a monumental beauty that is rivaled by few other gorges.

The upper reaches of Forbidding Canyon attract the occasional explorer with enough skill, stamina, and equipment to negotiate its spectacular but obstacle-strewn floor. Towering on either side of Forbidding Canyon are Cummings Mesa and Navajo Mountain. From the top of Cummings Mesa is one of the most magnificent views in the Navajo Country. Though the wilderness scene is now altered and partly obscured by the sinuous blue serpent of Lake Powell, enough remains to make this one of the most remarkable views anywhere—mile upon mile of canyon-gashed, billowing slickrock supporting a series of barren, sculptured buttes of orange-pink Entrada sandstone, whose glow in the light of sunset rivals even that of Monument Valley.

Navajo Mountain, its turtle-backed form rising in an even curve to more than 10,000 feet, is the highest point in the Navajo Country, and here, surrounded by the slickrock desert of the Rainbow Plateau, the mountain often catches—in fact, sometimes creates—its own crown of clouds, whose snow and rain water a forest of spruce, fir, and aspen, creating an island oasis in a sea of desiccation.

Until a few years ago the only way to claim the reward of a view from the top of Navajo Mountain was to climb it on foot or on horseback. Then in 1963, despite resistance to such a project's being undertaken by outsiders, some Navajo officials approved construction of a truck trail to the top of the mountain in order to install a radio relay station. The project went through, although it was opposed by the local Navajos, to whom the mountain is holy, being associated with one of the War Gods.

I climbed Navajo Mountain at the time when the road had reached the half-way point near War God Spring. When I descended from the summit I went by way of the road, and passed an old Navajo riding up it, chanting. Soon thereafter, I encountered a log and rock barrier blocking the road, and a little way farther on, another. A third followed, and a fourth, and a fifth. In this way one Navajo had registered his protest against an invasion of his holy mountain and the Reservation's remaining wilderness. At the last barrier, I found a note left by a traveler, who said he had grown so discouraged removing other barriers from below that point that he had given up; he wished those who followed better luck.

When one gains the top of Navajo Mountain, either by foot or by four-wheel-drive, he can look out over much of the Navajo Country. From different open places near the top of the mountain, he can see eastward across the Tsegi Mesas to the towers of Monument Valley and southward to Forbidding Canyon and Cummings Mesa. To the north and west, draped around the base of the mountain like a very wrinkled skirt, is the sandstone maze of the Baldrock Crescent. The intricacy of the carving of this wilderness of stone is beyond belief, and so is the scale of the landscape. The drop from mountaintop to canyon bottom was, before the reservoir, well over 7,000 feet; Rainbow Bridge's 309 feet are nearly, though not quite, lost in the labyrinth.

Of this "vast yellow and purple corrugated world of distance," Zane Grey said: "I imagined there was no scene in all the world to equal this. The tranquility of lesser spaces was here not manifest. . . . Sound, movement, life seemed to have no fitness here. Ruin was there and desolation and decay. The meaning of the ages was flung at me. A man became nothing. But when I gazed across that sublime and majestic wilderness, in which the Grand Canyon was only a dim line, I strangely lost my terror and something came to me across the shining spaces."

Although it is a forbidding country in many ways, it holds an irresistible fascination. There must be many cor-

ners in its fastness that have never been seen by non-Indians, nor perhaps, even by Indians. I have been, it seems likely, the first non-Indian to visit a natural arch that lies within sight of Rainbow Lodge Trading Post but which was previously unknown even to the trader there. Harold Quick, who was one of my companions on that occasion, spotted the difficult-to-see opening one morning as we were exploring the country south of the trading post. When we reached the arch, after an easy hike, we found on the floor of the cave behind it potsherds and a perfect white arrow point.

There must be arches in this wild land that no one has seen. Ruins too, and petroglyphs, and an infinite variety of fins, buttes, beehives, and gorges carved from cross-bedded Navajo sandstone, fifteen hundred feet thick. In places the land is split by deep narrow chasms which recall, in diminished form, the cathedral-like canyons drowned by Lake Powell. Here cool shaded alcoves draped with maidenhair fern still exist. Grottoes are lit by the wondrous orange glow of sunlight reflected from the cliffs opposite; and there are weeping walls, where the moisture from springs and seeps sustains miniature gardens amid miles of barrenness.

Anyone who follows the Rainbow Trail around Navajo Mountain and down into Cliff Canyon and Bridge Canyon crosses one of the wildest and weirdest landscapes in the world and can still recapture something of the thrill the first effective discoverers of Rainbow Bridge must have experienced when, in 1909, they rounded the last bend and first saw the bridge.

The Colorado and San Juan rivers were the northern and western boundaries of the Navajo Reservation's northwestern territory until they were lost in the rising reservoir behind Glen Canyon Dam and ceased to be rivers. The reservoir buried Glen Canyon and its innumerable canyon tributaries beneath billions of tons of water, destroying the canyon Zane Grey described as "too magnificent to be compared with others," drowning the best of the territory that inspired geologist Herbert E. Gregory, who knew this country as few men have, to write: "the region is seen to possess a ruggedness probably surpassed by few other parts of the world . . . it is difficult to conceive of an intricacy of canyon labyrinth and a variety of erosion remnants surpassing those exhibited by the Rainbow Plateau. . . . The intricacy and grandeur of the stream-carved sculpture are unexcelled in any other part of the Plateau province." Yet the still-rising reservoir waters have been allowed to penetrate mile after mile of these unique canyons, until, already, all but a pitifully few remnants have slipped silently beneath the surface of the

man-made lake. Gone are Dungeon, Labyrinth, Cathedral, Mystery, and the myriad other side canyons cut into the Navajo side of Glen Canyon. Gone is the haunting downward cadenza of the canyon wren in the cool shadows of Music Temple. Even Rainbow Bridge, which Theodore Roosevelt called the world's greatest natural wonder, would be threatened if the lake ever filled to capacity, for then the waters would be backed under the arch itself, to sap the strength of the rock on which the bridge is based, and silting beneath the bridge would put rubble and mud, not gold, at the foot of the Rainbow.

I recall the last time I saw Music Temple—in fact, probably the last time anyone saw it intact, for the waters of Lake Powell, then rising about two feet a day, had filled the channel of the small dry wash that drained the alcove, though they hadn't quite reached the still, dark pool in the Temple's interior. The outer edges of the sandbar in front of the alcove already had been eaten away, and chunks of sand continued to fall with dismal plopping sounds into the lake, leaving as a parting protest a dirty foam on the water's surface. Those parts of the bar that still had a few hours left before meeting their fate were gay with flowers—red, pink, and white—blooming fiercely, taking their last opportunity to add color to the world.

[*Oliver LaFarge, in Laughing Boy*]

He was riding the hundred miles from T'o Tlakai to Tsé Lani to attend
a dance, or rather, for the horse-racing that would come afterwards.
The sun was hot and his belly was empty, but life moved in rhythm
with his pony loping steadily as an engine down the miles. He was lax
in the saddle, leaning back, arm swinging the rope's end in time to the
horse's lope. His new red headband was a bright colour among the
embers of the sunstruck desert, undulating like a moving graph of the
pony's lope, or the music of his song—

> *Nashdui bik'e dinni, eya-a, eyo-o . . .*
> Wildcat's feet hurt *eya-a, eyo-o . . .*

Rope's end, shoulders, song, all moved together, and life flowed
in one stream. He threw his head back to sing louder, and listened to
the echo from the cliffs on his right. He was thinking about a bracelet he
should make, with four smooth bars running together, and a turquoise
in the middle—if he could get the silver. He wished he could work
while riding; everything was so perfect then, like the prayers, *hozoji
nashad*, travelling in beauty. His hands, his feet, his head, his insides
all were *hozoji*, all were very much alive. He whooped and struck up the
Magpie Song till the empty desert resounded—

> *A-a-a-ine, a-a-a-ine,*
> *Ya-a-ine-aine, ko-ya-aine . . .*

He was lean, slender, tall, and handsome, Laughing Boy, with a new cheap
headband and a borrowed silver belt to make ragged clothes look fine.

. . .

Almost best of all was to sit on a knoll, smoking and watch the animals feed.
One never sees a horse so well as when he is grazing close by, intent upon the grass,
oblivious of the man. Then one sees how he moves his ears, how he blows through
his soft nostrils, how his casual movements are made. He moves from clump to
clump, making his selections by standards of his own, never still, yet entirely free
of the restlessness of a stalled horse. It is the essence of pastoral life. Cigarette smoke
rises lazily in the hot air, the sun is comfortable upon one's bones, the gently
moving animals make peace. ◆

The horse's feet are mirage, his gait rainbow; sun strings his bridle, black rain his tail,
cloud with little rain his mane; his ears are of distant lightning, his eyes big star
twinkling, his teeth of white shell, his voice of black flute, his lips of large bead,
his face of vegetation, his belly of dawn.

Cottonwoods at mouth of Canyon de Chelly

At one end of the dance area, close enough to the bonfire to be comfortably warm after the night had taken on an edge, there was a big log. I sat on the end of it next to a middle-aged, grim-looking Indian, a man with the broad cheekbones, strong nose, and firm mouth of the true Apache type. You would say he was a formidable customer. Beyond him his wife was all but faceless in her blanket, watching the dance. The man had something under his blanket at which he looked from time to time. By and by he spoke to another, elderly Indian standing near him. The second Indian bent down to look, they both spoke softly and smiled. Then he spoke to a man behind him and the process was repeated. At length, after eyeing me a couple of times, pride was too much for him and he turned to me.

"Shoh," he said, "look how it sleeps."

He opened the blanket enough to let me see a baby, screwed up tight in sleep.

"It sleeps," he said, "very much it sleeps."

"Yes, very much it sleeps."

It was small and pink with a brown overcast, its features were more neatly cut, it was more attractive than white babies.

"How many its returning snows?" I asked.

"Nine moons."

"A boy? A girl?"

"A girl."

The man's smile was lovely. The Navajo behind us leaned forward to join our admiring. The father repeated softly, "Very much it sleeps," and touched its face gently with one finger. I did the same. We smiled at each other. The baby half-woke and let out a trial cry. Its mother turned, spoke sharply, the man closed his blanket and settled to watch the dance looking like any husband caught off base, the other Indian and I felt sheepish.

—OLIVER LaFARGE

Hogan, Canyon de Chelly

IX. Diné

THE NAVAJO Country is a land of a living people, the *Diné*. It is an old land, to them, and the people, their hogans and their herds of sheep seem a part of it.

Since the acquisition of livestock from the Spanish, the traditional Navajo way of life has been pastoral, based on sheep, with agriculture a supplement. Crafts are another old, though limited, source of income, and in the old days hunting and raiding were important activities. In this dry land the location of water limits possible locations for homes, although wells and the storage of water in tanks have in recent times permitted expansion of settlement.

Although increasing numbers of Navajos are building houses in conventional American style, the traditional round or octagonal, earth-covered, dome-shaped *hogan*, with the summer addition of a ramada, or shade, built of poles and brush, is still the common house. The hogan of First Man was built of sheets of sunbeam and rainbow, and the doorways of present hogans face east to receive the first blessing of the rising sun. Mythology stresses that every part of the hogan is sacred and that its interior as well as its surroundings must be kept clean and in good order. Great care must be taken in choosing a building site, and the structure must not intrude upon the landscape of which it is a part but must blend with the other local elements. As in every culture, however, practice doesn't always live up to the ideal, and not infrequently hogans are surrounded by scattered tin cans and glass. But the traditional hogan does blend with the land and, indeed, often seems almost a part of the natural scene, as does its owner and her flocks.

The herding life is not an easy one, especially in below-zero winter weather when snow may blanket the ground, and it requires a lot of country and constant wandering to find adequate feed for flocks where vegetation is sparse and thorny. Summer heat is less of a problem, for it is moderated by the 6,000-foot average elevation and the air is dry. However, temperatures above 100° are frequent in the lower areas, and rain and sometimes heavy hail often catch the herder, usually a woman, a child, or an old man, out in the open, far from shelter. The cutting and hauling of wood for cooking and heating are other outdoor activities that are arduous and never-ending, especially for Navajos who live far from areas where trees grow.

The dangers of nature are referred to in myth, some of them personified by the evil monsters of legend; the Rock That Claps Together, the Rock Monster That Kicks People Off, the Cutting Reed People, the Water Bug People, and Tracking Bear. It is important, however, that the monsters were born of the unnatural behavior by the people themselves. Though the worst of those monsters

were slain, their evil can never be completely conquered, and with their death the earth itself was contaminated. Fortunately, the good aspects of nature are here to aid and sustain man in his struggle with evil, and even the hardships of living close to nature make the Navajo more sensitive to its beauties. The word "beautiful" appears again and again in Navajo ritual, though it is, of course, not precisely the same concept among the Navajos as it is among the people of an Anglo-American culture. In Navajo the words for beauty and joy are the same, and an awareness and appreciation of nature's gifts inspires much of Navajo myth and ceremony. An example is this excerpt from the myth of the Mountaintop Way:

"Before him were the beautiful Big Mountain Sheep Peaks with their forested slopes. The clouds hung over the mountain, the showers of rain fell down its sides, and all the country looked beautiful. And he said to the land, 'Ahalani, greetings . . .'"

Frank Waters, a student of Navajo religion has written: ". . . as translations multiply, we are beginning to recognize the lyrics of the Navajo songs as pure poetry. Great poetry. Its rhythm sings even in the printed word. It abounds with metaphors and similes so subtle as to be almost incomprehensible to those who do not know the country and the intense feeling it evokes."

The Navajo are remarkably knowledgeable about the geography of their huge reservation. With allotments, it is larger than the state of West Virginia. Many Navajos have traveled widely in their land, and there is among them a pervasive interest in locality. Navajo place names are usually descriptive of the land; few commemorate people or events. Place names are most often simple, like *Tees Toh*, "Cottonwood Springs," but occasionally a more poetic name is encountered, such as *Kai Chineldlo*, "Willows Line Out Like Braids."

Though depending on repetition for much of its effect, Navajo ritual literature and mythology is full of arresting imagery. Haze, for example, is called the pollen of morning and evening sky. In the Male Shooting Way, buffalo are described as "moving with the sky as a mirage, black streak on the earth." The emphasis on nature in ritual is not for purely aesthetic reasons, of course, but is also for very practical purposes of influencing nature. Mist and dark clouds are referred to not only for their beauty and drama but also because their mention symbolizes rain and other gifts of nature and is meant to induce them.

Each wild animal has a place in the universal scheme. Religion still emphasizes the sacredness of the now rare game animals. The Navajo shows little religious respect toward the domesticated animals upon which he depends for food, however to him they are property, not sentient beings. In Navajo mythology there is great appreciation for wildflowers. Every plant is a symbol of vegetation, without which neither men nor animals could exist, and vegetation is considered the dress of the earth, a gift bestowed at creation and a function of Changing Woman's (Earth's) annual rejuvenation. The Navajo have a strong feeling for plants, which they treat with the greatest respect.

The symbol for life and productivity, for peace and prosperity, is pollen. Pollen symbolizes light. The Navajo are very conscious of light and color, both of which abound in their homeland, and these are mentioned constantly in ritual.

The Navajo cosmogony teaches that the earth should not be injured. From the earth man takes his life. When the earth is ill, its sickness is transmitted to man, and steps must be taken to restore harmony. Man must maintain himself in harmony with nature, reëstablish this harmony once lost, or perish.

Though the philosophy is there, lack of familiarity with scientific concepts often prevents its being translated into effective practice by the Navajo—and by all non-Navajos as well. Appalling overgrazing has led to destruc-

tion of much of the range, with consequent wind and water erosion, but most graziers have failed to see the relationship between overgrazing and this destruction of land. They consider that current situations—for example, the erosion of arroyos—are not the result of something that is presently occurring, but rather, of something that has already occurred. Present channel-cutting is thought to be the result of some past disharmony between man and nature, and thus present removal of excess stock, or herding flocks in another fashion, would have no influence on the face of the land. Although well-educated people are aware of the relationships between overgrazing and damage to the land, the problem still persists—in Navajo Country and almost everywhere else.

The grazing and overgrazing that has gone on for generations almost everywhere in Navajo Country has had major effects on vegetation, and for this reason there are few areas of significant size in the Navajo Country that are true wilderness. There are, however, some vast, roadless, "quasi-wilderness" areas in the northwestern part of the Reservation, and here one ten-mile-long island mesa, No Man's Mesa, may be a virtually untouched fragment of environment. Elsewhere, where the extreme ruggedness of the northwest is lacking, population pressure has pushed roads and two-track truck trails into even the most remote corners of the country. Still, most of these roads are unobtrusive examples of their kind, and much of the country celebrates nature's hand, not man's.

Earth, for it I am ashamed.
Sky, for it I am ashamed.
Evening, for it I am ashamed.
Blue sky, for it I am ashamed.
Darkness, for it I am ashamed.
Sun, for it I am ashamed.
In me it stands, with me it talks, for it I am ashamed.
—DECLARATION OF THE SINGER, ORIGIN LEGEND

Restore all for me in beauty,
Make beautiful all that is before me.
Make beautiful all that is behind me.
Make beautiful my words.
It is done in beauty.
It is done in beauty.
It is done in beauty.
It is done in beauty.
—PRAYER, MOUNTAINTOP WAY

Chinle formation, Beautiful Valley

South end of Monument Valley

It is characteristic of Indians when not under overwhelming pressure that they never lose sight of the great, fundamental question: *What makes life worth living?* This is one of the factors which makes white men find them exasperating to deal with, for our theory of profit is extremely simple and so deeply rooted that we cannot understand a man who decides that under the circumstances the money offered is not worth the sacrifices or efforts demanded for it. The Apaches understand this very well and they, above all the Apaches of Navajo, selected from what they saw around them only what suited their intentions.

—Oliver La Farge

It is lovely indeed, it is lovely indeed.
I, I am the spirit within the earth . . .
The feet of the earth are my feet . . .
The legs of the earth are my legs . . .
The bodily strength of the earth is my bodily strength . . .
The thoughts of the earth are my thoughts . . .
The voice of the earth is my voice . . .
The feather of the earth is my feather . . .
All that belongs to the earth belongs to me . . .
All that surrounds the earth surrounds me . . .
I, I am the sacred words of the earth . . .
It is lovely indeed, it is lovely indeed.

—Song of the Earth Spirit, Origin Legend

Canyon of Aztec Creek above junction with Bridge Canyon

The people walk over me.
The old men all say to me, I am beautiful . . .
—THE CHANT OF THE BEAUTIFUL MOUNTAINS OF EAST AND WEST

On trail between Bridge Canyon and Oak Canyon

Waterfall, trail to Keet Seel Ruin, Navajo National Monument

In beauty may I dwell.
In beauty may I walk.
In beauty may my male kindred dwell.
In beauty may my female kindred dwell.
In beauty may it rain on my young men.
In beauty may it rain on my young women.
In beauty may it rain on my chiefs.
In beauty may it rain on us.
In beauty may our corn grow.
In the trail of pollen may it rain.
In beauty before us may it rain.
In beauty behind us may it rain.
In beauty below us may it rain.
In beauty above us may it rain.
In beauty all around us may it rain.
In beauty may I walk.

—PRAYER, NIGHT WAY

Among them I walk.
I speak to them;
They hold out their hands to me.
—SONG OF THE LONG POT

[*Oliver LaFarge, Enemy Gods*]

The enrolling clerk at Tsaili Boarding School mopped his brow with his sleeve.
It was very hot in early September; the room, overcrowded with children, was stifling.

'All right, next,' he said.

Bido Tso, the policeman, shoved forward another frightened little boy. His hand
on the child's shoulder was firm, not rough, and he spoke to him kindly in Navajo.
The clerk looked at the boy. Thin and big-eyed, the kind that gets T.B. and dies
on you. His long hair was utterly untidy, he wore a torn cotton shirt, very dirty
calico leggings, and moccasins which were coming to pieces.

'What's his name?' the clerk asked wearily.

'Ashin Tso-n Bigé. It's his fadder's name. He's dead.'

'His father's called Ushin Tsone Begay?'

'No, dat's dis one. He's his son. It's his fadder's name, his son.'

The policeman meant that the boy was called Ashin Tso-n's Son, but the clerk
was too harassed, and spoke no Navajo.

'Hell,' he said. 'He's Begay, hunh?'

The policeman gave up. 'Yes.'

'Begay. What'll we call him, Miss Sparks?'

The first-grade teacher looked at the poor little rat. 'Call him Myron,' she said.
'It kinda suits him.'

'Myron Begay, then.' The clerk started again. 'Age—humm—six. First grade.
Your name is Myron, see? Where's he from?'

'Beykashi-ha-Bik'é.'

'Oh Lord! What's that near?'

'Joneses store.'

'Home address, Joneses Trading Post. All right, next.'

The policeman told the boy, 'They will call you Mylon, you understand,
grandchild? When they say that, "Mylon," you come.'

The child started without speaking, hardly comprehending. He was pushed on.
The policeman was used to this, he had become toughened to it. Big Salt's Son.
That man had been a leader, a person of distinction. Well, that's how the whites are.
He brought up a little girl, who was crying.

. . .

Events had been bewildering since the boy found himself in the crowded truck jouncing over the ungraded road. The bewilderment increased progressively in rate. He never did get the next period of time straight in memory; it remained blurred, intentionally obliterated later, a matter for casual joking when one was an older boy, a shock never really forgotten. Under a variety of hands, along with other children some of whom wept, some struggled, some were stolid, he passed through swift and astounding treatments. There were white voices and faces and the white language, bursts of laughter and grunts of effort. The Field Matron and Boys' Matron in uniforms, the Disciplinarian—an Indian face, but strange, not Navajo—others. He was held, his hair cut, shorn, like a sheep, he was stripped, scrubbed, deloused, passed from person to person, examined swiftly and none too thoroughly by a rough-handed doctor, clothed again, and at length turned loose in the sunshine through another door.

For a brief space he wandered blindly, trying to recover his scattered integrity. Casual personal contact revolts the Indian, handling is offensive, even a stepchild has recognized personality, a right to his dignity. It seemed as if there were nothing left of himself to gather up. His crop-head felt uncovered, naked. His clean blue work-shirt, too large for him and turned up at the cuffs, and very old, clean blue overalls were not entirely strange as a costume, but the shoes confounded his walking. Heavy, ill-fitting, hard leather boxes, high-laced, prison-made at Leavenworth, and of none too good quality, shipped in thousands by an erratically thrifty government to weight down feet accustomed to the soft lightness of moccasins. Unconsciously the boy walked with an awkward, unnecessary lift of the weights which would characterize his gait for some years to come.

The formation of lines and military march into the dining room were not very successful. No one expected they would be. Later the children would move with routine perfection, but now the staff was exhausted by the little ones and still dreading the next few days' mess. The newcomers faced the strangeness of a huge hall in which a hundred and seventy sat down to eat, and the novelty of tables, chairs, knives, forks and spoons. They were too miserable and too shy for food, only a few even fiddled with the coffee.

. . .

After supper there was a bare, ill-lit room with scuffed and splintered floor and a few backless, wooden benches, the common room, where in winter overcoats and sweaters were hung. Older children played outside while the Disciplinarian and Boys' Matron set to undressing the dozen little boys and putting them to bed. Toothbrushing was not attempted at this time; the rushing water and the dark, wet, semi-subterranean lavatory terrified some of the children as it was.

In the dormitory were seventy-five beds for a total of ninety boys. The iron frames, in need of paint and with springs sagging, stood in rank on rank, twelve inches apart. On a rail at the foot of each, its occupant hung his clothes. Two enormous stoves, empty now, loomed in the room for winter heating, the floor around them and from them to the door was smudged black with coal dust and ashes. From time to time a few new beds or new mattresses were secured to replace the most completely ruined, the rest continued in service like lame soldiers.

Myron stared with deep depression at this great, homeless cavern and the unending iron frames and dark, army blankets. Limply he climbed into his assigned place beside Jack Tease. The two of them lay still for a long time, as did the others. Then the older children came to bed in disciplined quietness and the lamps were blown out. There was a slight, hushed movement in the dormitory. The boldest of the newcomers slipped to the ground and rolled up in their blankets under their beds, finding some sense of protection there. Here and there a child cried in the privacy of darkness. An older boy whispered a hasty word of comfort in Navajo, his eye cocked toward the Disciplinarian's door. Slowly the place became silent.

. . .

He stood still. He was by the corner of the hospital, where the ground fell away into the dry wash. Ahead of him he could see the wide sweep of desert, then the great wall of Black Mesa and the peak he knew so well; far away, tremendous distances for a little boy, far enough to be rather blue at noontide. The space between was a whole unknown world to traverse. He looked around. No one was in sight. He slid into the arroyo.

He was out of bounds now, but it could appear to be only play. He occupied himself picking up brightly coloured stones, moving quietly, listening intently. No one had noticed. He worked his way along the dry river-bed to the bend. Then he ran. His leaping heart stopped him finally. Breathless and with his face burning hot, he crawled into shade and partial hiding under a cut-bank, lying close against the sand. He could not make himself wait there long, only until his lungs came under control, then he set out, plodding, and a little farther along climbed up the west bank with infinite precaution.

Behind a quarter of a mile of scattering greasewood and chamisa the red-brick buildings stared at him. He crouched, frightened by their malignant dominance. He crawled a way, then walked bent over till a rise of ground cut off even the slate rooftops and long chimneys. The sun hovered just above the edge of Black Mesa, which was turning to a deep blue and rising higher, closer, in the evening sky. Tlichisenili reached out to him. Steady, determined, he walked, no taller than the bushes, a tiny figure of seriousness on the face of the desert. ◆

Dunes near Sand Springs, Monument Valley

Today I will walk out, today everything evil will leave me, I
will be as I was before, I will have a cool breeze over my body,
I will have a light body.

. . .

I will be happy forever, nothing will hinder me;
I walk with beauty before me, I walk with beauty behind me, I walk
    with beauty below me, I walk with beauty above me, I walk
    with beauty around me, my words will be beautiful;
        —PRAYER, MYTH OF BEAUTY WAY FEMALE BRANCH

Roof Butte, Chuska Mountains

He is like the Most-High-Power-Whose-Ways-Are-Beautiful.
With beauty before him,
With beauty behind him,
With beauty above him,
With beauty below him,
All around him is beautiful.
His spirit is all beautiful.

—CHANT FOR PROTECTION FROM DISEASE

Limestone boulders, Marble Gorge

Epilogue

THERE WAS a chill in the night air on the summit of the Chuskas as the fire died down to embers. The moon added no warmth nor did the stars, and I was drawing the sleeping bag more closely about me when I caught a faint sound. A slight shifting of the gentle wind that still stirred the pines momentarily brought it closer—voices, clearly now, in a high-pitched chanting. There was something alien about it yet also something elemental, and I shivered. My ears strained to hear more, and now and again the sound was clear for several long moments, only to fade as the breeze shifted or died. I wondered whether the song was part of a Night Way or some other curing ceremony. I thought of legends these songs recount, legends of monsters and heroes, of animate and inanimate nature, of humanity; and I realized that to the singers of these songs, man and nature and the supernatural were not separate but rather were parts of a single great continuum. The monsters are the dangerous and unpleasant aspects of man and nature that result from disharmony, and the heroes are the beneficent and pleasant. The basic dichotomy was between good and evil, not between man and nature.

The breeze brought back the chant, mingled it for the moment with the calling of an owl. A faint fragrance of smoke from distant campfires mixed with the pine smell, the pines, and my bed of needles felt comfortable and secure. For a moment I envied the life of the Navajos, never cut off from nature, but part of it and it of them. In a pastoral fantasy I visualized myself as natural man, one of the heroes of legend, living with the good earth.

But for that blissful moment I had forgotten the monsters—the cold of winter, the starving time, the time of disease and death. The land that fills the soul does not always fill the belly; the low productivity of the land forces isolation on its occupants, and human companionship suffers. The adversities of nature and society can't provide the challenge that keeps us truly alive, but they can also overwhelm us.

So where does the balance lie? Certainly some of the answer is to be found in the pines that surrounded me, even in the bitter cold of the Navajo winter. Yet would many men really abandon the prizes of centuries of human struggle: great art and music; secure, comfortable, and beautiful dwellings; a wide variety of companionship; easy transportation to the far corners of the earth; modern medicine; and a broad choice of different ways of life?

We know the dangers and disadvantages of urbanization, even at its best, and we know too that too much security robs us of something vital. Perhaps the non-Indian can learn from the Navajo tradition of continuity with nature just as the Navajo is learning about modern technological society. The contrast adds zest to both. Urban man, although freed from many of nature's demands, he nevertheless senses an uneasy alienation from the elements to which he is biologically adapted. A return to the wilderness has a special poignancy even though it may take time to readjust to a half-forgotten way of living. And when one reënters the urban world it can be appreciated anew. Perhaps man will some day reconcile the greatness of his human creativity with the greatness of the wild that created it. If we can do this without diminishing either man's great works or nature's, then we shall indeed walk in beauty for as long as the rivers shall run and the grass shall grow.

In beauty may I walk.
All day long may I walk.
Through the returning seasons may I walk.
Beautifully will I possess again.
Beautifully birds . . .
Beautifully joyful birds . . .
On the trail marked with pollen may I walk.
With grasshoppers about my feet may I walk.
With dew about my feet may I walk.
With beauty may I walk.
With beauty before me may I walk.
With beauty behind me may I walk.
With beauty above me may I walk.
With beauty all around me may I walk.
In old age wandering on a trail of beauty, lively, may I walk.
In old age wandering on a trail of beauty, living again, may I walk.
If it finished in beauty.
It is finished in beauty.

—Prayer, Night Way

A field of mallow near rim of Marble Gorge

That flowing water! That flowing water! My mind wanders across it.

That broad water! That flowing water! My mind wanders across it.

That old age water! That flowing water! My mind wanders across it.

—MYTH OF THE MOUNTAINTOP WAY

[*Willa Cather, Death Comes for the Archbishop*]

Father Latour had used to feel a little ashamed that Joseph kept his sister and her nuns so busy making cassocks and vestments for him; but the last time he was in France he came to see all this in another light. When he was visiting Mother Philomène's convent, one of the younger Sisters had confided to him what an inspiration it was to them, living in retirement, to work for the faraway missions. She told him also how precious to them were Father Vaillant's long letters, letters in which he told his sister of the country, the Indians, the pious Mexican women, the Spanish martyrs of old. These letters, she said, Mother Philomène read aloud in the evening. The nun took Father Latour to a window that jutted out and looked up the narrow street to where the wall turned at an angle, cutting off further view. "Look," she said, "after the Mother has read us one of those letters from her brother, I come and stand in this alcove and look up our little street with its one lamp, and just beyond the turn there, is New Mexico; all that he has written us of those red deserts and blue mountains, the great plains and the herds of bison, and the canyons more profound than our deepest mountain gorges. I can feel that I am there, my heart beats faster, and it seems but a moment until the retiring-bell cuts short my dreams."

. . .

When the summer wind stirred the lilacs in the old gardens and shook down the blooms of the horse-chestnuts, [Father Latour] sometimes closed his eyes and thought of the high song the wind was singing in the straight, striped pine trees up in the Navajo forests.

During the day his nostalgia wore off, and by dinnertime it was quite gone. He enjoyed his dinner and his wine, and the company of cultivated men, and usually retired in good spirits. It was in the early morning that he felt the ache in his breast; it had something to do with waking in the early morning. It seemed to him that the grey dawn lasted so long here, the country was a long while in coming to life. The gardens and the fields were damp, heavy mists hung in the valley and obscured the mountains; hours went by before the sun could disperse those vapours and warm and purify the villages.

In New Mexico he always awoke a young man; not until he rose and began to shave did he realize that he was growing older. His first consciousness was a sense of the light dry wind blowing in through the windows, with the fragrance of hot sun and sage-brush and sweet clover; a wind that made one's body feel light and one's heart cry "To-day, to-day," like a child's.

Beautiful surroundings, the society of learned men, the charm of noble women, the graces of art, could not make up to him for the loss of those light-hearted mornings of the desert, for that wind that made one a boy again. He had noticed that this peculiar quality in the air of new countries vanished after they were tamed by man and made to bear harvests. Parts of Texas and Kansas that he had first known as open range had since been made into rich farming districts, and the air had quite lost that lightness, that dry aromatic odour. The moisture of plowed land, the heaviness of labour and growth and grain-bearing, utterly destroyed it; one could breathe that only on the bright edges of the world, on the great grass plains or the sage-brush desert.

· · ·

Marble Gorge of Grand Canyon at site of proposed Marble Canyon dam

That air would disappear from the whole earth in time, perhaps; but long after his day. He did not know just when it had become so necessary to him, but he had come back to die in exile for the sake of it. Something soft and wild and free, something that whispered to the ear on the pillow, lightened the heart, softly, softly picked the lock, slid the bolts, and released the prisoned spirit of man into the wind, into the blue and gold, into the morning, into the morning!